Encou

3-MINUTE DEVOTIONS
FOR WOMEN

Daily Encouragement

3-MINUTE DEVOTIONS FOR WOMEN

BARBOUR BOOKS
An Imprint of Barbour Publishing, Inc.

Introduction

Most days we're seeking out a moment or two of inspiration and encouragement—a fresh breath of air for the lungs and soul.

Here is a collection of moments from the true Source of all inspiration and encouragement—God's Word. Within these pages you'll be guided through just-right-size readings you can experience in as few as three minutes:

- Minute 1: Reflect on God's Word
- Minute 2: Read real-life application and encouragement
- Minute 3: Pray

These devotions aren't meant to be a replacement for digging deep into the scriptures or for personal, in-depth quiet time. Instead, consider them a perfect jump start to help you form a habit of spending time with God every day. Or add them to the time you're already spending with Him. Share these moments with friends, family, coworkers, and others you come in contact with every day. They're looking for inspiration and encouragement too.

Your word is a lamp to guide
my feet and a light for my path.
PSALM 119:105 NLT

Day 1

RENEWED HOPE AND FAITH

I am Alpha and Omega, the beginning
and the end, the first and the last.
REVELATION 22:13 KJV

In the Old Testament, the Lord God called Himself a Shepherd, the Alpha and Omega, the Beginning and the End, and the Almighty. He is called the First and the Last. In the New Testament, we find the same titles given to Jesus. The Bible is unique because in it God fully reveals who He is. Since Jesus is fully God, let it renew our hope and faith in our Savior. He who created all things out of nothing will re-create this world into a paradise without sin.

Jesus, I learn how to live by Your human
example, and I trust in You as my God—Father,
Son, and Holy Spirit—three persons,
one God, one perfect You! Amen.

Day 2

GOD'S PROMISES BRING HOPE

"For I know the plans I have for you...
plans to prosper you and not to harm you,
plans to give you hope and a future."
JEREMIAH 29:11 NIV

The writer of the well-known hymn "It Is Well with My Soul" penned those words at the most grief-stricken time of his life after his wife and three children were tragically killed at sea. His undaunted faith remained because he believed in a God who was bigger than the tragedy he faced. God's promises gave him hope and encouragement. Despite your circumstances, God has a plan for you, one that will give you encouragement and hope and a brighter future.

Father, may I always say, "It is well with
my soul," knowing Your promises are true
and I can trust You no matter what.

Day 3

EXPECTANT HOPE

*In the morning, LORD, you hear my voice; in the morning
I lay my requests before you and wait expectantly.*
PSALM 5:3 NIV

God fulfills His side of the bargain to hear our prayers.
Then we take off on our merry way, trying to solve our
dilemma without Him. We leave His presence without
lingering with the Lord to listen and to worship Him in
the silence of our heart. Then later we return with more
demands and "gimmes." God knows our human hearts
and understands. He gently waits to hear from us—and He
delights when we keep our end of the bargain and linger
in His light with hearts full of anticipation and hope.

*Dear God, my hope is in You. Thank You for
listening to my prayers and knowing exactly
what I need. I wait patiently, expectantly,
knowing You will answer me. Amen.*

Day 4

SEEKING GOD'S PLAN

For we are His workmanship, created in
Christ Jesus for good works, which God prepared
beforehand that we should walk in them.

EPHESIANS 2:10 NKJV

How can you know God's plans for your life? First, you should meet with Him in prayer each day and seek His will. Studying the Bible is also important. Often, God speaks to us directly through His Word (Psalm 119:105). Finally, you must have faith that God *will* work out His plan for your life and that His plan is good. Jeremiah 29:11 (NIV) says, " 'For I know the plans I have for you,' declares the LORD, 'plans to prosper you and not to harm you, plans to give you hope and a future.' " Are you living in Christ's example and seeking God's plan for your life?

Father, what is Your plan for me? I know it is good.
Reveal it to me, Lord. Speak to me through prayer.

Day 5

BEHIND THE SCENES

*Now faith is confidence in what we hope for
and assurance about what we do not see.*
HEBREWS 11:1 NIV

Be encouraged today that no matter what takes place in the natural—what you see with your eyes—it doesn't have to be the final outcome of your situation. If you've asked God for something, then you can trust He is working out all the details behind the scenes. What you see right now, how you feel, is not a picture of what your faith is producing. Your faith is active, and God is busy working to make all things come together and benefit you.

Heavenly Father, what I see today is not what I'm going to get. Thank You for working behind the scenes to bring about the very best for my life. Amen.

Day 6

ROCK SOLID

"Therefore everyone who hears these words of mine and puts them into practice is like a wise man who built his house on the rock. The rain came down, the streams rose, and the winds blew and beat against that house; yet it did not fall, because it had its foundation on the rock."

MATTHEW 7:24–25 NIV

Prepare for tomorrow's storms by laying a solid foundation today. Rain and wind are guaranteed to come. It is only a matter of time. We need to be ready. When our foundation is the Rock, Jesus Christ, we will find ourselves still standing when the storm has passed. Rain will come. Winds will blow and beat hard against us. Yet, when our hope is in the Lord, we will not be destroyed. We will remain steadfast because our feet have been firmly planted. Stand upon the Rock today so that your tomorrows will be secure.

Dear Lord, help me build my foundation today upon You so I can remain steadfast in the storms of life. Amen.

Day 7

JOYFUL, PATIENT, AND FAITHFUL

Be joyful in hope, patient in affliction,
faithful in prayer.
ROMANS 12:12 NIV

Faithfulness in prayer requires discipline. God is faithful regardless of our attitude toward Him. He never changes, wavers, or forsakes His own. We may be faithful to do daily tasks around the house. We feed the cat, wash the clothes, and empty the trash. But faithfulness in the quiet discipline of prayer is harder. There are seemingly no consequences for neglecting our time with the Lord. Oh, what a myth this is! Set aside a daily time for prayer and see how the Lord blesses you, transforming your spirit to increase your joyful hope, your patience, and your faithfulness.

Faithful God, find me faithful. Stir up the
hope and joy within me. Give me the
grace I need to wait on You. Amen.

Day 8

A MATTER OF PRIORITIES

To everything there is a season,
a time for every purpose under heaven.
ECCLESIASTES 3:1 NKJV

Only one thing in our lives never changes: God. When our world swirls and threatens to shift out of control, we can know God is never surprised, never caught off guard by anything that happens. Just as He guided David through dark nights and Joseph through his time in prison, God can show us a secure way through any difficulty. He can turn the roughest times to good. Just as He supported His servants in times past, He will always be with us, watching and loving.

Lord, help me remember Your love and guidance
when my life turns upside down. Grant me wisdom
for the journey and a hope for the future. Amen.

Day 9

UNSWERVING FAITH

*Let us hold unswervingly to the hope
we profess, for he who promised is faithful.*

HEBREWS 10:23 NIV

The author of Hebrews challenges us to hold *unswervingly* to our hope in Christ Jesus. Certainly we fail to do this at times, but life is much better when we keep our eyes fixed on Him. Sometimes just a whisper from Satan, the father of lies, can cause shakiness where once there was steadfastness. Place your hope in Christ alone. He will help you to resist the lies of this world. Hold *unswervingly* to your Savior today. He is faithful!

*Jesus, You are the object of my hope. There are
many distractions in my life, but I pray that
You will help me to keep my eyes on You.
Thank You for Your faithfulness. Amen.*

Day 10

DAYBREAK

"As your days, so shall your strength be."
DEUTERONOMY 33:25 NKJV

There are times in life when we feel that the night season we're facing will last forever and a new morning will never come. For those particularly dark seasons of your life, you don't have to look to the east to find the morning star, but instead find that morning star in your heart. Allow the hope of God's goodness and love to rekindle faith. With the passing of the night, gather your strength and courage. A new day is dawning and with it new strength for the journey forward. All that God has promised will be fulfilled.

*Heavenly Father, help me to hold
tightly to faith, knowing in this situation
that daybreak is on its way. Amen.*

Day 11

WEARY DAYS

Why art thou cast down, O my soul? and why art thou disquieted in me? hope thou in God: for I shall yet praise him for the help of his countenance. O my God, my soul is cast down within me: therefore will I remember thee from the land of Jordan, and of the Hermonites, from the hill Mizar.

PSALM 42:5–6 KJV

Our willingness to speak with God at the day's beginning shows our dependence on Him. We can't make it alone. It is a comforting truth that God never intended for us to trek through the hours unaccompanied. He promises to be with us. He also promises His guidance and direction as we meet people and receive opportunities to serve Him. Getting started is as simple as removing our head from beneath the pillows and telling God good morning.

Lord, refresh my spirit and give me joy for today's activities. Amen.

Day 12

IT'S ALL GOOD

And we know that all things work together for
good to them that love God, to them who are
the called according to his purpose.

ROMANS 8:28 KJV

God can and does use all things in our lives for His good purpose. Remember Joseph in the cistern, Daniel in the lions' den, and Jesus on the cross? The Lord demonstrated His resurrection power in each of those cases. He does so in our lives as well. He brings forth beauty from ashes.

What are you facing that seems impossible? What situation appears hopeless? What circumstance is overwhelming you? Believe God's promise.

Dear Lord, thank You that You work all things
together for Your good purpose. May I trust
You to fulfill Your purpose in my life. Amen.

Day 13

LORD, HELP!

"LORD, help!" they cried in their trouble, and he saved them from their distress. He calmed the storm to a whisper and stilled the waves. What a blessing was that stillness as he brought them safely into harbor!
PSALM 107:28–30 NLT

Samuel Morse, the father of modern communication, said, "The only gleam of hope, and I cannot underrate it, is from confidence in God. When I look upward it calms any apprehension for the future, and I seem to hear a voice saying: 'If I clothe the lilies of the field, shall I not also clothe you?' Here is my strong confidence, and I will wait patiently for the direction of Providence." The answer to your prayer does not depend on you. Your expressions of your heart spoken to your Father bring Him onto the scene for any reason you need Him.

Father, thank You for hearing my prayers. I know that You are always near to me and You answer my heart's cry. Help me to come to You first instead of trying to do things on my own.

Day 14

THE GIFT OF ENCOURAGEMENT

We have different gifts. . . . If it is to encourage,
then give encouragement.
ROMANS 12:6, 8 NIV

Paul spoke of encouraging as a God-given desire to proclaim God's Word in such a way that it touches hearts to move them to receive the Gospel. Encouragement is a vital part to witnessing because encouragement is doused with God's love. For the believer, it stimulates our faith to produce a deeper commitment to Christ. It brings hope to the disheartened or defeated soul. It restores hope. How will you know your spiritual gift? Ask God and then follow the desires He places on your heart.

Father, help me tune in to the needs of those
around me so that I might encourage them for
the Gospel's sake for Your glory and their good.

Day 15

OPEN THE BOOK

For everything that was written in the past was written to teach us, so that through the endurance taught in the Scriptures and the encouragement they provide we might have hope.
ROMANS 15:4 NIV

Life is tough. We get discouraged and, at times, disheartened to the point of such despair it's hard to recover. Reading *all* of God's Word is paramount. It is the source of hope, peace, encouragement, salvation, and so much more. It moves people to take action while diminishing depression and discouragement. As the writer of Hebrews put it, "For the word of God is alive and active. Sharper than any double-edged sword…" (Hebrews 4:12 NIV). Need some encouragement? Open the Book.

Lord, help me read Your Word consistently to empower me with the hope and encouragement I need.

Day 16

PASS IT ON!

*After the usual readings from the books of Moses
and the prophets, those in charge of the service sent
them this message: "Brothers, if you have any word of
encouragement for the people, come and give it."*

ACTS 13:15 NLT

Encouragement brings hope. Have you ever received
a word from someone that instantly lifted your spirit?
Did you receive a bit of good news or something that
diminished your negative outlook? Perhaps a particular
conversation helped to bring your problems into
perspective. Paul passed on encouragement and many
benefited. So the next time you're encouraged, pass it
on! You may never know how your words or actions
benefited someone else.

*Lord, thank You for the wellspring of
encouragement through Your holy Word.*

Day 17

A BOLD REQUEST

When they had crossed, Elijah said to Elisha,
"Tell me, what can I do for you before I am taken
from you?" "Let me inherit a double portion
of your spirit," Elisha replied.

2 KINGS 2:9 NIV

What a bold request.

Elijah filled the role of leader, prophet, and miracle worker. Why would Elisha want the heavy responsibilities and difficulties involved in this type of work? He did not ask to have a larger ministry than Elijah—he was only asking to inherit what Elijah was leaving and to be able to carry it on.

What might God give us if we asked boldly for the impossible? God deeply desires to bless us. If our hearts line up with His will and we stay open to His call, He will surprise us. God takes the ordinary and through His power transforms our prayers into the extraordinary— even double-portion requests.

Bless me, Lord. When my heart aligns with Your will
and when I ask for the impossible, bless me. Show me
beyond my expectations that You are my God. Amen.

Day 18

A LITTLE GOES A LONG WAY

*"The LORD our God has allowed a few
of us to survive as a remnant."*

 EZRA 9:8 NLT

Remnants. Useless by most standards, but God is in the business of using tiny slivers of what's left to do mighty things. Nehemiah rebuilt the fallen walls of Jerusalem with a remnant of Israel; Noah's three sons repopulated the earth after the flood; four slave boys—Daniel, Shadrach, Meshach, and Abednego—kept faith alive for an entire nation. When it feels as if bits and pieces are all that has survived of your hope, remember how much God can accomplish with remnants!

*Father God, thank You for proving that there
is hope. . .even in the remnants! Amen.*

Day 19

LORD OF THE DANCE

Remember your promise to me; it is my only hope.
PSALM 119:49 NLT

The Bible contains many promises from God: He will protect us (Proverbs 1:33), comfort us (2 Corinthians 1:5), help in our times of trouble (Psalm 46:1), and encourage us (Isaiah 40:29). The word *encourage* comes from the root phrase "to inspire courage." Like an earthly father encouraging his daughter from backstage as her steps falter during her dance recital, our Papa God wants to inspire courage in us, if we only look to Him.

Promise Keeper, You are the one true source of courage. Thank You for Your promises and for giving me courage when I need it most.

Day 20

GO FOR IT

When everything was hopeless,
Abraham believed anyway, deciding to
live. . .on what God said he would do.
ROMANS 4:18 MSG

"You can't do that. It's impossible." Have you ever been told this? Or just thought it because of fear or a previous experience with failure? This world is full of those who discourage rather than encourage. If we believe them, we'll never do anything. But if we, like Abraham, believe that God has called us for a particular purpose, we'll go for it despite our track records. Past failure doesn't dictate future failure. If God wills it, He fulfills it.

Help me to have the faith of Abraham,
Father God. . .to believe anyway!

Day 21

CHERISHED DESIRE

God our Father loves us. He is kind and has given us
eternal comfort and a wonderful hope.
2 THESSALONIANS 2:16 CEV

Webster's definition of hope: "To cherish a desire with expectation." In other words, yearning for something wonderful you expect to occur. Our hope in Christ is not just yearning for something wonderful, as in "I hope for a sunny beach day." It's a deep trust with roots that extend from the beginning of time to the infinite future. Our hope is not just the anticipation of heaven, but the expectation of a fulfilling life walking beside our Creator and best Friend.

Dear heavenly Father, I want to journey through life
in hopeful expectation—always anticipating
You'll work in wonderful ways!

Day 22

FEEL THE LOVE

Long before he laid down earth's foundations,
he had us in mind, had settled on us as the focus
of his love, to be made whole and holy by his love.
EPHESIANS 1:4 MSG

Need a boost of hope today? Read this passage aloud, inserting your name for each "us." Wow! Doesn't that bring home the message of God's incredible, extravagant, customized love for you? I am the focus of His love, and I bask in the hope of healing, wholeness, and holiness His individualized attention brings. You too, dear sister, are His focus. Allow yourself to feel the love today.

Long before You laid down earth's foundations,
You had me in mind, had settled on me as the
focus of Your love, to be made whole and holy
by Your love. Thank You, Jesus! Amen.

Day 23

MAKEOVER

*Since I was worse than anyone else, God had
mercy on me and let me be an example
of the endless patience of Christ Jesus.*
1 TIMOTHY 1:16 CEV

Saul was a Jesus hater. He went out of his way to hunt
down believers to torture, imprison, and kill. Yet Christ
tracked him down and confronted him in a blinding
light on a dusty road. Saul's past no longer mattered.
Previous sins were forgiven and forgotten. He was
given a fresh start. A life makeover. We too are offered
a life makeover. Christ offers to create a beautiful new
image of Himself in us, unblemished and wrinkle-free.

*Thank You for new beginnings and fresh starts,
God. You have erased my sins, and now
I walk free in Your unending grace!*

Day 24

HOW SHOULD I TALK TO GOD?

"This, then, is how you should pray: 'Our Father in heaven, hallowed be your name, your kingdom come, your will be done, on earth as it is in heaven. Give us today our daily bread. And forgive us our debts, as we also have forgiven our debtors. And lead us not into temptation, but deliver us from the evil one.'"

MATTHEW 6:9–13 NIV

Jesus gave us an example of how to pray in His famous petition that was recorded in Matthew 6:9–13. We don't need to suffer with an anxious heart or feel ensnared by this world with no one to hear our cry for help. We can talk to God, right now, and He will listen. The act of prayer is as simple as launching a boat into the Sea of Galilee, but it's as miraculous as walking on water.

God, how wonderful it is that You hear me when I call out to You and that You answer with exactly what I need. Amen.

Day 25

WHICH WAY DO I GO?

I will instruct you and teach you in the way you should go; I will counsel you with my loving eye on you.

Psalm 32:8 niv

God says, "I will instruct you and teach you in the way you should go; I will counsel you with my loving eye on you." That is truly what we need in a noisy world that may offer little reliable or usable advice. God not only promises to guide us, to teach us the way we should go, but He plans on doing it with a loving eye on us. For the most loving counsel, listen to the voice of God. He's talking to you, and He has something important to say that will change your life.

Wonderful Counselor, help me to be receptive to Your voice and to always trust in Your guidance. Amen.

Day 26

HE WILL ANSWER

*I waited patiently for the LORD; and he inclined
unto me, and heard my cry. He brought
me up also out of an horrible pit.*

PSALM 40:1–2 KJV

David found himself trapped in a "horrible pit" with
no apparent way out, and he cried loudly to the Lord
to rescue him. Then he waited. It took time for God to
answer. David undoubtedly learned more patience in the
process and probably had to endure doubts, wondering
if God cared about the dilemma he was in.

Even Jeremiah didn't always get immediate answers
to prayer. One time he and some Jewish refugees were
in a dire situation and were desperate to know what to
do. Yet after Jeremiah prayed, the Lord took ten days to
answer (Jeremiah 42:7). But the answer *did* come. . .in time.

Today we sometimes find ourselves in a "horrible
pit" as well, and we pray desperately for God to bring
us up out of it. He will. We often just need to be patient.

*Why is patience so hard? It's because Your timing
is perfect and beyond my understanding.
Help me to be patient with You, God. Amen.*

Day 27

HARM FOR GOOD

"You meant evil against me, but God meant it for good."
GENESIS 50:20 NASB

Joseph suffered more in his lifetime than any of us ever will. But God remembered him, blessed him, and made him a man of great authority in the land so that he was in the position to make wise decisions and save many people from starvation.

Instead of feeling entitled to apologies, Joseph wanted redemption in place of revenge. In response to his brothers' wanting security, he replied, "Don't be afraid. Am I in the place of God? You intended to harm me, but God intended it for good to accomplish what is now being done, the saving of many lives" (Genesis 50:19–20 NIV).

Maybe you're in the middle of suffering right now, so deep in it you can't possibly see any good. Take encouragement from Joseph's words. You are not God—you cannot see what He sees. Maybe yet there will be some good that comes out of the harm.

Dear God, help me to trust in Your plans. Amen.

Day 28

WHAT TO DO WITH FREE WILL

"If you do what is right, will you not be accepted?
But if you do not do what is right, sin is crouching
at your door; it desires to have you,
but you must rule over it."

GENESIS 4:7 NIV

Every single thing we do every minute of the day involves a choice, and everything has a ripple effect. Everything has consequences. What we eat for breakfast. What books we read, what programs we watch on TV. Where we go, what we spend our time and money on. Sin is always crouching at our door, but with the help of the Holy Spirit we can tell it to leave. What will your choices be today?

Holy Spirit, guide me in my decisions. Help me to
be wise, clearheaded, and motivated by a
selfless love for You and others. Amen.

Day 29

THE TIME IS NOW

But God demonstrates His own love toward us,
in that while we were yet sinners, Christ died for us.
ROMANS 5:8 NASB

In the book of Mark, Jesus said, "The time has come.... The kingdom of God has come near. Repent and believe the good news!" (1:15 NIV). Have you embraced this good news? The kingdom of God has come near to you. Why are you waiting? The time is now. Ask the Lord for forgiveness and be free. Believe in Him as Lord and be made right with God. Accept His grace and live with the Lord for all time. Oh yes, what a joy—to know love the way it was meant to be!

Thank You, Lord Jesus, that even while I was deep in my sin, You gave up Your life so that I might truly live. What a sacrifice. What a Savior! Thank You for Your unfathomable mercy, Your immeasurable love. Amen.

Day 30

TREMBLING WHILE TRUSTING

*And straightway the father of the child cried out,
and said with tears, Lord, I believe;
help thou mine unbelief.*

MARK 9:24 KJV

When the Lord looks at us, what does He see? Do we trust Him enough to be vulnerable? Are we willing to obey even when we are afraid? Do we believe Him? Do not be afraid to follow Him, and do not let your trembling hold you back. Be willing to take a step of faith. If you are scared, God understands and is compassionate and merciful. Fear does not negate His love for you. Your faith will grow as you trust Him. Let's trust even while trembling.

*Dear Lord, help my unbelief. Enable me to trust You
even though I may be trembling. Amen.*

Day 31

GET REAL

The Lord says: "These people come near to me with their mouth and honor me with their lips, but their hearts are far from me. Their worship of me is based on merely human rules they have been taught."

ISAIAH 29:13 NIV

The world is full of hypocrites. To be honest, sometimes the church is too—hypocrites who profess to know and honor God, but when it comes right down to it, they are only going through the motions of religion. Their hearts are far from Him. Take the time to find out who God is, what He has done for you, and why He is worthy of your devotion. Following God is not about a bunch of man-made rules. He loves you; He sent His Son to die for you; and He longs to have a deep, personal relationship with you. Get real with God and get real with yourself!

Dear God, reveal Yourself to me. Show me who You are, and show me how to live so that I honor You not only with my lips but with my heart as well. Amen.

Day 32

GOD IS DOING SOMETHING NEW

"See, I am doing a new thing! Now it springs up;
do you not perceive it? I am making a way in
the wilderness and streams in the wasteland."
ISAIAH 43:19 NIV

Imagine that desert, dry and barren—with no hope of even a cactus flower to bloom—suddenly coming to life with bubbling pools of pure water. That is what God promises us. He is doing something new in our lives. He is making a path through what feels impassable, and He will command a stream to flow through the wilderness of our pasts, places where we had only known the wasteland of sin and a landscape of despair. Have faith and bring your empty buckets to the stream.

Father, thank You for Your provision, hope, and joy.
Without You, life is dry and hostile. Come into my
life and quench my thirst. You are the only
One who can fulfill me. Amen.

Day 33

THE ANSWER IS NO ONE

The LORD is my light and my
salvation—whom shall I fear?
PSALM 27:1 NIV

When you accept Christ as your Savior, you get certain things in return. You get an understanding of good and evil—and you get the knowledge that you are on the side of good. You get a clearer vision of the darkness in your life—and you get a Friend who is always with you, no matter how dark things seem to be. And you get peace—through knowing your place before God. That you stand in His grace, blameless and pure, and you have a place in heaven created just for you. A place no one can take away.

Dear Jesus, help me to feel You at my side. Amen.

Day 34

I THINK I CAN

"Do not be afraid; only believe."
MARK 5:36 NKJV

Take a trip through the Bible and you'll see that those God asked to do the impossible were ordinary people of their day; yet they demonstrated that they believed God saw something in them they didn't see. He took ordinary men and women and used them to do extraordinary things. When you believe you can do something, your faith goes to work. You rise to the challenge, which enables you to go further than before, to do more than you thought possible. Consider trying something new—if you think you can, you can!

God, I want to have high expectations. I want to do more than most think I can do. Help me to reach higher and do more as You lead me. Amen.

Day 35

WHAT'S IN YOUR HEART?

Delight thyself also in the LORD: and he shall
give thee the desires of thine heart.

PSALM 37:4 KJV

Too many times we look at God's promises as some sort of magic formula. We fail to realize that His promises have more to do with our own relationship with Him. It begins with a heart's desire to live your life in a way that pleases God. Only then will fulfillment of His promises take place. The promise in Psalm 37:4 isn't intended for personal gain—it is meant to glorify God. God wants to give you the desires of your heart when they line up with His perfect plan. As you delight in Him, His desires will become your desires, and you will be greatly blessed.

Lord, I know You want to give me the desires of my
heart. Help me live in a way that makes this possible.

Day 36

MY LIFE

*I long for your salvation, L*ORD*, and your law
gives me delight. Let me live that I may praise
you, and may your laws sustain me.*

PSALM 119:174–175 NIV

Can you really do laundry to please God? Can you really
go to work to please God? Can you really pay the bills and
make dinner to please God? The answer is a resounding
yes! Doing all the mundane tasks of everyday life with
gratitude and praise in your heart for all that He has
done for you is living a life of praise. As you worship
God through your day-to-day life, He makes clear His
plans, goals, and dreams for you.

*Dear Father, let me live my life to praise You.
Let that be my desire each day. Amen.*

Day 37

GOD CARES FOR YOU

"Consider how the wild flowers grow. They do not labor or spin. Yet I tell you, not even Solomon in all his splendor was dressed like one of these. If that is how God clothes the grass of the field, which is here today, and tomorrow is thrown into the fire, how much more will he clothe you—you of little faith!"

LUKE 12:27-28 NIV

If God makes the flowers, each type unique and beautiful, and if He sends the rain and sun to meet their needs, will He not care for you as well? He made you. What the Father makes, He loves. And that which He loves, He cares for. We were made in His image. Humans are dearer to God than any of His other creations. Rest in Him. Trust Him. Just as He cares for the birds of the air and the flowers of the meadows, God is in the business of taking care of His sons and daughters. Let Him take care of you.

Father, I am amazed by Your creation. Remind me that I am Your treasured child. Take care of me today as only You can do. Amen.

Day 38

BE STILL

*Thou wilt keep him in perfect peace, whose mind
is stayed on thee: because he trusteth in thee.*
ISAIAH 26:3 KJV

Longing for His children to know His peace, God sent prophets like Isaiah to stir up faith, repentance, and comfort in the hearts of the "chosen people."

God's message is just as applicable today as it was back then. By keeping our minds fixed on Him, we can have perfect, abiding peace even in the midst of a crazy world. The path to peace is not easy, but it is simple: Focus on God. As we meditate on His promises and His faithfulness, He gets bigger, while our problems get smaller.

*God, when I focus on the world, my mind and heart
feel anxious. Help me to keep my mind on
You so that I can have hope and peace.*

Day 39

HE HAS CHOSEN YOU

Therefore, as God's chosen people, holy and dearly loved, clothe yourselves with compassion, kindness, humility, gentleness and patience.

COLOSSIANS 3:12 NIV

No matter how athletic, beautiful, popular, or smart you are, you've probably experienced a time when you were chosen last or overlooked entirely. Being left out is a big disappointment of life on earth. The good news is that this disappointment isn't part of God's kingdom. Even when others forget about us, God doesn't. He has handpicked His beloved children now and forever. The truth is that Jesus died for *everyone*—every man, woman, and child who has ever lived and will ever live. The Father chooses us all. All we have to do is grab a glove and join the team.

Father, thanks for choosing me. I don't deserve it, but You call me Your beloved child. Help me to remember others who may feel overlooked or unloved. Let Your love for them shine through me. Amen.

Day 40

SETTING PRIORITIES

Cause me to hear Your lovingkindness in the morning,
for in You do I trust; cause me to know the way in
which I should walk, for I lift up my soul to You.
PSALM 143:8 NKJV

Twenty-four hours. That's what we all get in a day. Though
we often think we don't have time for all we want to do,
our Creator deemed twenty-four-hour days sufficient. How
do we decide what to devote ourselves to? The wisdom
of the psalmist tells us to begin the day by asking to hear
the loving voice of the One who made us. We can lay our
choices, problems, and conflicts before Him in prayer.
He will show us which way to go. Psalm 118:7 (NIV) says,
"The LORD is with me; he is my helper." Hold up that full
plate of your life to Him and allow Him to decide what
to keep and what to let go.

Lord, make me willing to surrender my choices
and activities to You. Cause me to desire
the things You want me to do.

Day 41

THE BREATH OF GOD

*Every part of Scripture is God-breathed and
useful one way or another—showing us truth,
exposing our rebellion, correcting our
mistakes, training us to live God's way.*
2 TIMOTHY 3:16 MSG

Do you spend time in God's Word each day? Do you let
the breath of God wash over you and comfort you? Are
you allowing His Word to penetrate your heart and show
you where you've been wrong? If not, you are missing
out on one of the most important ways God chooses to
communicate with us today. Ask the Lord for the desire
to spend more time in His Word. Don't feel you have the
time? Consider purchasing an audio Bible and listen to
God's Word as you drive to work or school.

*Father, Your Word is so important to me.
Please give me the desire to spend more
time in the Bible each day. Amen.*

Day 42

CONFIDENCE

*For I know that my redeemer liveth, and that he
shall stand at the latter day upon the earth:
and though after my skin worms destroy
this body, yet in my flesh shall I see God.*
JOB 19:25–26 KJV

Although we experience various difficulties throughout life, we can still look forward to the blessed future we have. No matter what our struggles are, our Lord controls. Job had no idea what the purpose of his trial was, but he faced his troubles with confidence, knowing that ultimately he would emerge victorious. Too many times we view our own situations with self-pity rather than considering God's strength and trusting that His plan is perfect. What peace God offers when we finally cast our cares on Him and with great conviction declare, "I know that my redeemer liveth"!

*O great Redeemer, in You I have confidence
even when I don't understand life's trials.
Please help me to live victoriously.*

Day 43

ALWAYS THINKING OF YOU

*What is man that You are mindful of him,
and the son of man that You visit him?*
PSALM 8:4 NKJV

Have you ever wondered what God thinks about? *You* are always on His mind. In all you think and do, He considers you and makes intercession for you. He knows the thoughts and intents of your heart. He understands you like no other person can. He knows your strengths and weaknesses, your darkest fears and highest hopes. He's constantly aware of your feelings and how you interact with or without Him each day. God is always with you, waiting for you to remember Him—to call on Him for help, for friendship, for anything you need.

*Lord, help me to remember You as I go throughout
my day. I want to include You in my life and
always be thinking of You too. Amen.*

Day 44

ALL YOU NEED

"For your Maker is your husband—the LORD Almighty is his name—the Holy One of Israel is your Redeemer; he is called the God of all the earth."

ISAIAH 54:5 NIV

God is the great "I Am." He is all things we need. He is our Maker. He is our Husband. He is the Lord Almighty, the Holy One, the Redeemer, the God of all the earth. . . . He is not a god made of stone or metal. He is not unreachable. He is present. He is near, as close as you will let Him be, and He will meet your needs as no earthly relationship can. Seek the fullness of God in your life. Call upon Him as your Prince of Peace and your King of Glory. He is all that you need—at all times—in all ways.

O Father, be close to me. Fill the empty spots in my heart. Be my Husband, my Redeemer, and my best Friend. Amen.

Day 45

CAN YOU HEAR ME NOW?

But as for me, I watch in hope for the LORD,
I wait for God my Savior; my God will hear me.
MICAH 7:7 NIV

If there's anything more frustrating than waiting for someone who never shows, it's trying to talk to someone who isn't listening. It's as if they have plugged their ears and nothing penetrates. Mothers are well acquainted with this exercise in futility, as are wives, daughters, and sisters. But the Bible tells us that God hears us when we talk to Him. He shows up when we wait for Him. He will not disappoint us.

When I talk, Lord, I know You will listen.
You will never let me down.

Day 46

POUR OUT PRAYERS

*Trust in Him at all times, you people; pour out your
heart before Him; God is a refuge for us.*
PSALM 62:8 NKJV

The psalmist tells us to trust the Lord at all times and to
pour out our hearts to Him. There is nothing we think
or feel that He does not already know. He longs for us
to come to Him, spilling out our thoughts, needs, and
desires. God invites us to an open-ended conversation.
He made us for relationship with Him. He never tires of
listening to His children. The Lord is our helper. He is
our refuge. He knows the solutions to our problems and
the wisdom we need for living each day.

*Lord, remind me of Your invitation to pour out my
problems to You. You are my refuge and my helper.
Help me to trust You with every detail of my life.*

Day 47

SOLITARY PRAYER

Come near to God and he will come near to you.
JAMES 4:8 NIV

Do you have a prayer closet?

In Matthew 6 Jesus warned against people praying in public with the intent to show others how pious they are. Instead, He advocated solitude. Jesus often went off by Himself to draw near to His Father and pray, and that is what He suggested in the passage from Matthew.

A secret room isn't necessary—rather a quiet place where one can be alone with God. Maybe your quiet place is your garden or the beach. It might be in the quiet of your own home when your husband and children are away. Wherever it is, enjoy some time alone with God. Draw near to Him in prayer, and He will draw near to you.

Dear God, when we meet in the quiet place,
allow me to breathe in Your presence. Amen.

Day 48

OBJECT OF FAITH

"And as Moses lifted up the serpent in the wilderness, even so must the Son of Man be lifted up, that whoever believes in Him should not perish but have eternal life."

JOHN 3:14–15 NKJV

When Nicodemus inquires of Jesus how a man receives eternal life, Jesus recalls this Old Testament image. Knowing He would be lifted up on a cross, the Lord Jesus points Nicodemus and us to faith in Him alone. We must repent of our sin and believe in the Son of God who died on the cross. Sin and its consequences are around us like serpents, but into the midst of our fallen world God has sent Jesus to save us. He is the object of our faith. The crucified and resurrected Christ is the answer. He is the truth, the way, and the life.

Father, fix my gaze on Your Son lifted up for me.

Day 49

I LIFT MY EYES

I lift up my eyes to the mountains—where does my help come from? My help comes from the Lord, the Maker of heaven and earth.
PSALM 121:1-2 NIV

Adulthood is a time when decisions can be the most crucial. Challenges, failures, doubts, and fears may cloud decisions and cripple us into inaction because the end result is unknown. Career paths, relationships, and financial decisions are only some of the areas that cause concern. In all of those things, and in all of life, we shouldn't keep our eyes fixed on the end result, and we shouldn't keep our heads down and simply plow through. Instead, we must lift our eyes to the Lord. If we fix our focus on Jesus, we will see He is prepared to lead and guide us through all of life's challenges.

Lord, I lift up my eyes to You. Please help me and guide me down the path of life. Let me never become so focused on my own goals or so busy about my work that I forget to look to You, for You are my help. Amen.

Day 50

MORNING ORDERS

"Have you ever given orders to the morning, or shown the dawn its place, that it might take the earth by the edges and shake the wicked out of it?"

JOB 38:12–13 NIV

God poses many rhetorical questions, all to show the might and wonder and mystery of the Almighty. In these words are some amazing ideas that really cause us to stop and consider who God is. And that is what we should do, especially when we face our worst trials. Stop and consider who God is. That no matter what happens, He will not leave us. And that He alone has the answers for us.

Thank You, God, for providing glimpses of You in Your Word. Amen.

Day 51

STILLNESS

Be still, and know that I am God.
PSALM 46:10 NKJV

David wrote, "Meditate within your heart on your bed, and be still" (Psalm 4:4 NKJV). Many of us have lost the ability to meditate on God. We either tell ourselves that meditation is something only Buddhist monks do, or else we cry out frantic prayers while distracted by the careening roller coaster of life. When we lie down in bed at night, instead of meditating calmly and trusting in God, we fret and toss and turn.

When we learn to trust that God can protect us and work out our problems, then we can lie down peacefully and sleep (Psalm 4:8). That same trust gives us the strength to face our days with confidence.

Dear God, quiet my mind. Remove from it all the worldly thoughts that come between You and me. Create stillness within me and turn my thoughts toward You. Amen.

Day 52

SENSE OF BELONGING

"All that the Father gives Me will come to Me, and the one who comes to Me I will by no means cast out."

JOHN 6:37 NKJV

We belong to Christ. When the Father calls us to come to Jesus, we belong to Him. This is an irrevocable transaction. We are His, given to Him by the Father. He does not refuse to save us. He will not refuse to help us. No detail of our lives is unimportant to Him. No matter what happens, He will never let us go. Like the enduring love of a parent—but even more perfect—is the love of Christ for us. He has endured all the temptations and suffered all the pain that we will ever face. He has given His very life for us. We can live peacefully and securely knowing we belong to Him.

Lord Jesus, I confess I often forget I belong to You and how much You love me. Help me to rest in Your everlasting love and care. Amen.

Day 53

LOOK UP!

The heavens declare the glory of God;
the skies proclaim the work of his hands.
PSALM 19:1 NIV

Grace is as near as the sky over your head. Look up and be reminded of how wonderful God truly is. The same God who created the sun and the atmosphere, the stars and the galaxies, the same God who day by day creates a new sunrise and a new sunset, that same God loves you and creates beauty in your life each day!

Father, when I look to the heavens, I am reminded
that You are Creator, Giver of grace, and Author
of beauty. Thank You for surrounding me
with the work of Your hands. Amen.

Day 54

FOLLOW JESUS

*"Whoever serves me must follow me; and where
I am, my servant also will be. My Father
will honor the one who serves me."*

JOHN 12:26 NIV

A disciple is someone who follows. That is the discipline
we practice: We follow Jesus. Wherever He is, we go. In
His presence we find the daily grace we need to live. As
we serve Him, God honors us; He affirms our dignity
and makes us all we were meant to be.

*Jesus, I long to be Your disciple. Give me the grace to
follow You, a heart to serve You, and a mind in tune
with You every minute of every day. Amen.*

Day 55

CHOSEN

"I have chosen you and have not rejected you."
ISAIAH 41:9 NIV

The Lord doesn't dump us when we don't measure up. And He doesn't choose us one minute only to reject us a week later. We need not fear being deserted by our loving Father. He doesn't accept or reject us based on any arbitrary standards. He loves us with an everlasting love (Jeremiah 31:3). By His own mercy and design, "he hath made us accepted in the beloved" (Ephesians 1:6 KJV).

Father, thank You that I don't need to
fear Your rejection of me. Amen.

Day 56

BY HIS GRACE

A person is made right with God through faith,
not through obeying the law.

ROMANS 3:28 NCV

Human laws can never make us into the people we are meant to be. No matter how scrupulous we try to be, we will always fall short. Our hands and hearts will come up empty. But as we fix our eyes on God, committing our lives and ourselves to Him, we are made right. We are healed and made whole by His grace, exactly as God meant us to be.

Father, rather than working to become righteous in
Your sight, help me instead to focus on increasing
my faith and trusting in Your grace. Amen.

Day 57

SAFE

*My life is in your hands. Save me from my enemies
and from those who are chasing me.*

PSALM 31:15 NCV

Do you ever feel like trouble is chasing you? No matter how fast you run or how you try to hide, it comes relentlessly after you, dogging your footsteps, breathing its hot breath down your neck, robbing you of peace. What's even worse is that it waits for you down the road as well! Maybe you need to stop running and hiding and instead let yourself drop into God's hands, knowing He will hold your future safe.

*Lord, when I am afraid, my instinct is to run.
Thank You for this reminder that my life is in Your
hands. Keep me safe. Help me to be still. Amen.*

Day 58

SPIRIT OXYGEN

Tell me this one thing: How did you receive the Holy Spirit? Did you receive the Spirit by following the law? No, you received the Spirit because you heard the Good News and believed it.

GALATIANS 3:2 NCV

As we share the good news of Christ, we need to take care that we are not preaching the law rather than the love of Christ. The Spirit did not come into your heart through legalism and laws—and He won't reach others through you if that is your focus. Breathe deeply of grace, and let it spread from you to a world that is desperate for the oxygen of the Spirit.

Father, Son, and Holy Spirit, how grateful I am for the good news of the Gospel. Remind me of the grace I have received and enable me to share it freely with others. Amen.

Day 59

DAILY MIRACLES

"That is why I tell you not to worry about everyday life—whether you have enough food and drink, or enough clothes to wear. Isn't life more than food, and your body more than clothing?"
MATTHEW 6:25 NLT

With our eyes fixed on what we don't have, we often overlook the grace we have already received. God has blessed us in many ways. Our bodies function day after day in amazing ways we take for granted, and life is filled with an abundance of daily miracles. Why do we worry so much about the details when we live in such a vast sea of daily grace?

Father, You are my Provider. You have promised to give me everything I need. Help me to remember this truth and to lose myself in the vast sea of Your amazing grace. Amen.

Day 60

HIS HEALING ABUNDANCE

"Behold, I will bring it health and healing;
I will heal them and reveal to them the
abundance of peace and truth."
JEREMIAH 33:6 NKJV

If we confess our sins to God, He will bring relief to our souls. When we're distressed, we have Jesus, the Prince of Peace, to give us peace. When our emotions threaten to overwhelm us, we can implore Jehovah Rapha—the God Who Heals—to calm our anxious hearts. When we're physically sick, we can cry out to Jesus, our Great Physician. Whether our problems affect us physically, spiritually, mentally, or emotionally, we can trust that God will come to us and bring us healing. And beyond our temporal lives we can look forward with hope to our heavenly lives. There we will be healthy, whole, and alive—forever.

Jehovah Rapha, thank You for healing me.
Help me do my part to seek health and the
abundance of peace and truth You provide.

Day 61

THY WILL BE DONE

He went away a second time and prayed, "My Father,
if it is not possible for this cup to be taken away
unless I drink it, may your will be done."

MATTHEW 26:42 NIV

Jesus didn't ask this once—He made this request three times in Matthew 26. These red-letter prayers reveal the 100 percent human side of Jesus.

In one of His darkest hours, Jesus was overwhelmed with trouble and sorrow. He asked God for something God would not provide. But Jesus, perfect and obedient, ended His prayers by saying, "*Your* will be done."

When we face our darkest hours, will we follow Jesus' example? Can we submit to God's perfect will, focusing on how much He loves us—even when His will doesn't match ours?

I wonder why You refuse when I ask for what I think
is right. But Your knowledge is greater than
my understanding. So Thy will be done,
God, Thy perfect will be done. Amen.

Day 62

HEALED PAST

"All their past sins will be forgotten, and they will live because of the righteous things they have done."

 EZEKIEL 18:22 NLT

We have the feeling that we can't do anything about the past. We think all our mistakes are back there behind us, carved in stone. But God's creative power is amazing, and His grace can heal even the past. Yesterday's sins are pulled out like weeds, while the good things we have done are watered so they grow and flourish into the present. Give your past to God. His grace is big enough to bring healing even to your worst memories.

Father, how grateful I am that my past is forgiven and I am free! Help me trust You to bring righteousness into my life. Amen.

Day 63

VALUABLE

*Better to be patient than powerful; better to have
self-control than to conquer a city.*
PROVERBS 16:32 NLT

Our world values visible power. We appreciate things like
prestige and skill, wealth and influence. But God looks at
things differently. From His perspective, the quiet, easily
overlooked quality of patience is far more valuable than
any worldly power. Patience makes room for others' needs
and brokenness. Patience creates a space in our lives for
God's grace to flow through us.

*Lord, when I come to Your Word, I am constantly
reminded that Your wisdom is not the world's
wisdom. Give me Your perspective. Draw me
toward the practice of patience. Amen.*

Day 64

WHOLE AND HEALTHY

*When Jesus heard this, he told them, "Healthy people
don't need a doctor—sick people do. I have come to
call not those who think they are righteous,
but those who know they are sinners."*

MARK 2:17 NLT

With Jesus, we never need to pretend to be something we
aren't. We don't need to impress Him with our spiritual
maturity and mental acuity. Instead, we can come to Him
honestly, with all our neediness, admitting just how weak
we are. When we do, we let down the barriers that keep
Him out of our hearts. We allow His grace to make us
whole and healthy.

*Jesus, help me to resist the temptation to be something
I'm not. Instead, give me a spirit of vulnerability.*

Day 65

LAVISH AND ABUNDANT

Let them come back to GOD, who is merciful,
come back to our God, who is lavish with forgiveness.
ISAIAH 55:7 MSG

God's forgiveness is never stingy or grudging. And He never waits to offer it to us. Instead, it's always there, a lavish, abundant flood of grace, just waiting for us to turn away from our sin and accept it.

Lord, when I am consumed by sin, my back is turned to
You. Thank You for Your mercy and lavish forgiveness
that gently turn me toward Your loving arms. Amen.

Day 66

AN ALL-THE-TIME THING!

*Pray diligently. Stay alert, with your
eyes wide open in gratitude.*
COLOSSIANS 4:2 MSG

Prayer is not a sometimes thing. It's an all-the-time thing!
We need to pray every day, being careful to keep the lines
of communication open between God and ourselves all
through the day, moment by moment. When we make
prayer a habit, we won't miss the many gifts of grace that
come our way. And we won't forget to notice when God
answers our prayers.

*Father, although it's important to set aside specific
time for prayer, I am reminded of the value
of being in constant communication with
You—my good Father, my Companion. Amen.*

Day 67

WELCOME INTERRUPTIONS

So they left by boat for a quiet place,
where they could be alone.

MARK 6:32 NLT

Jesus and the disciples sought a quiet place, away from the crowds. Like us, they needed alone time. But as so often happens, people interrupt those moments of solitude. The crowd follows us, the phone rings, someone comes to the door. When that happens, we must ask Jesus for the grace to follow His example and let go of our quiet moments alone, welcoming the interruption with patience and love.

Jesus, I am good at setting my own agenda.
Help me to see life's interruptions as gifts from You,
rather than disruptions to my "perfect" plan. Amen.

Day 68

RIGHT NOW

For God says, "At just the right time, I heard you.
On the day of salvation, I helped you." Indeed,
the "right time" is now. Today is the day of salvation.
2 Corinthians 6:2 nlt

God always meets us right now, in the present moment. We don't need to waste our time looking over our shoulders at the past, and we don't have to feel as though we need to reach some future moment before we can truly touch God. He is here now. Today, this very moment, is full of His grace.

Lord, make me mindful of Your presence right
now, in this very minute. You have redeemed my
past, and You hold my future in Your hands.
This moment is the one I must cling to. Amen.

Day 69

FROM THE INSIDE OUT

*Take on an entirely new way of life—a God-fashioned
life, a life renewed from the inside and working
itself into your conduct as God accurately
reproduces his character in you.*

EPHESIANS 4:24 MSG

At the end of a long week, we sometimes feel tired and
drained. We need to use feelings like that as wake-up
calls, reminders that we need to open ourselves anew
to God's Spirit so He can renew us from the inside out.
Grace has the power to change our hearts and minds,
filling us with new energy to follow Jesus.

*Lord, the world says change comes from the
outside. Your Word says that true transformation
comes from the inside. Meet me there—on
the inside—and make me like You. Amen.*

Day 70

SATISFIED

*Satisfy us in the morning with your unfailing love,
that we may sing for joy and be glad all our days.*
PSALM 90:14 NIV

God wants to fulfill you. He wants you to feel satisfied
with life so you will catch yourself humming or singing
His praises all day long. Even when life is hard, He is
waiting to comfort you with His unfailing love so that
gladness will creep over your heart once more.

*Father, You are the Author of joy. Thank You so much
for Your unfailing love that fills me to the brim. Give me
grace and gladness every minute of every day. Amen.*

Day 71

A QUIET PACE

"Teach me, and I will be quiet.
Show me where I have been wrong."

JOB 6:24 NCV

Do you ever feel as though you simply can't sit still?
That your thoughts are swirling so fast that you can't
stop them? That you're so busy, so stressed, so hurried
that you have to run, run, run? Take a breath. Open your
heart to God. Allow Him to quiet your frantic mind. Ask
Him to show you how you can begin again, this time
walking to the quiet pace of His grace.

Father, quietness does not always come easily.
The frenetic pace of this world sucks me in.
Fill my lungs with Your breath. Quiet me
and help me to be still. Amen.

Day 72

TAKE A BREAK

*"Only in returning to me and
resting in me will you be saved."*
ISAIAH 30:15 NLT

Some days you try everything you can think of to save
yourself, but no matter how hard you try, you fail again
and again. You fall on your face and embarrass yourself.
You hurt the people around you. You make mistakes,
and nothing whatsoever seems to go right. When that
happens, it's time to take a break. You need to stop trying
so hard. Throw yourself in God's arms. Rest on His grace,
knowing He will save you.

*Father, sometimes I feel so unsure of myself.
Help me to relax, to rest in Your arms, and to
remember that You are my good teacher,
my support, and my comfort. Amen.*

Day 73

OUR CONFIDENCE

*Have no fear of sudden disaster or of the ruin
that overtakes the wicked, for the LORD will be at your
side and will keep your foot from being snared.*
PROVERBS 3:25-26 NIV

Whether our loved ones are in harm's way daily or
not, all of us live in a dangerous world. And while we
should take physical precautions, our best preparation
is spiritual. When we spend time with God and learn
about His love for us and our families, we begin to
realize He will give us His grace when we need it. He
promises never to leave us, and the more we come to
know His love, the more we will rest in that promise.

*God, thank You that You promise Your peace
to those who seek You. Help me to rest
in Your love for my family and me.*

Day 74

LIFE AND NOURISHMENT

*"I, the LORD, am the one who answers your prayers
and watches over you. I am like a green pine
tree; your blessings come from me."*
HOSEA 14:8 NCV

Think of it: God is like a tree growing at the center of
your life! In the shade of this tree you find shelter. This
tree is evergreen, with deep roots that draw up life and
nourishment. Each one of life's daily blessings is the
fruit of this tree. It is the source of all your life, all your
joy, and all your being.

*Lord, how can I thank You for answering my prayers
and watching over me? I am grateful for Your many
blessings and for You, the source of my being. Amen.*

Day 75

LIVING A COMPLETE LIFE

It is a good thing to receive wealth from
God and the good health to enjoy it.
ECCLESIASTES 5:19 NLT

God has promised to supply all your needs, but it takes action on your part. Seeking wisdom for your situation and asking God to direct you in the right decisions will help you find a well-balanced life that will produce success, coupled with the health to enjoy it. It may be as simple as realizing a vacation is exactly what you need, instead of working throughout the year and taking your vacation in cash to pay for new bedroom furniture. Know when to press forward and when to stop and enjoy the life God has given you for His good pleasure—and yours!

Lord, I ask for Your wisdom to help me balance my life
so I can be complete in every area of my life. Amen.

Day 76

PRAISE HIM!

"The LORD is my strength and song, and He has become my salvation; this is my God, and I will praise Him."
EXODUS 15:2 NASB

God makes you strong, He makes you sing with gladness, and He rescues you from sin. These are the gifts of His grace. When He has given you so much, don't you want to give back to Him? Use your strength, your joy, and your freedom to praise Him.

Father, Your Word tells me You have armed me with strength! This is such a gift. Help me to use this strength to honor You. Amen.

Day 77

ADORNED WITH GRACE

Don't ever forget kindness and truth.
Wear them like a necklace.
PROVERBS 3:3 NCV

Kindness and truth are strands of the same necklace.
You should not be so kind that you evade the truth, nor
should you be so truthful that you wound others. Instead,
adorn yourself with both strands of this necklace. Wear
it with grace.

Father, there exists such a perfect balance between
kindness and truth. One without the other would not
be enough. Give me grace to be kind and
boldness to be truthful. Amen.

Day 78

CHRIST BALANCE

*Jesus caught them off balance with his own
test question: "What do you think about
the Christ? Whose son is he?"*

MATTHEW 22:41-42 MSG

Sometimes Christ asks us to find new ways of thinking
. . .new ways of living. . .new ways of encountering Him
in the world around us. That is not always easy. We don't
like to be caught off balance. When our life's equilibrium
is shaken, we feel anxious, out of control. But if we rely
on Christ, He will pick us up, dust us off and give us the
grace to find our balance in Him.

*Dear Jesus, sometimes I think I have things all figured
out; then You ask a hard question. When I am thrown
off balance, steady me with Your truth. Amen.*

Day 79

NEW INSIGHT

*Your word is a lamp to guide my
feet and a light for my path.*
PSALM 119:105 NLT

We sometimes take scripture for granted. These ancient words, though, continue to shine with light just as they did centuries ago. In them, God's grace is revealed to us. In them, we gain new insight into ourselves and our lives.

Father, every time I open Your Word, I am blessed by a fresh revelation of Your truth. May Your ancient words drip like sweet honey into the depths of my soul. Amen.

Day 80

REDEMPTION

*Put your hope in the Lord, for with the Lord is
unfailing love and with him is full redemption.*

PSALM 130:7 NIV

When God permits a redemption, or "buying back," of
lost years and relationships, we get a black-and-white
snapshot of the colorful mural of God's redemption of
us in Christ. When we one day stand in His presence,
we'll understand more clearly the marvelous scope of
God's redeeming love. In ways we cannot now begin
to imagine. In broken relationships we thought could
never be restored.

*I praise You, Father, for Your awesome redemption.
Thank You that I've yet to see the scope of it all. Amen.*

Day 81

THE MISSING PIECES

Trust the L<small>ORD</small> with all your heart,
and don't depend on your own understanding.
P<small>ROVERBS</small> 3:5 <small>NCV</small>

Life is confusing. No matter how hard we try, we can't always make sense of it. We don't like it when that happens, and so we keep trying to determine what's going on, as though we were trying puzzle pieces to fill in a picture we long to see. Sometimes, though, we have to accept that in this life we will never be able to see the entire image. We have to trust God's grace for the missing pieces.

Dear Lord, my own understanding is awfully limited,
and yet I still sometimes try to depend on it. Help me
to trust You with 100 percent of my heart. Amen.

Day 82

JUST WHAT WE NEED

*God can pour on the blessings in astonishing ways so
that you're ready for anything and everything, more
than just ready to do what needs to be done.*
2 Corinthians 9:8 MSG

Blessings are God's grace visible to us in tangible form.
Sometimes they are so small we nearly overlook them—
the sun on our faces, the smile of a friend, or food on the
table—but other times they amaze us. Day by day, God's
grace makes us ready for whatever comes our way. He
gives us exactly what we need.

*God, the more I see Your blessings, the more they seem
to pour out on me. Give me Your grace to receive
and eyes to see Your goodness. Amen.*

Day 83

REACH OUT TO HIM

*"Your words have supported those who were falling;
you encouraged those with shaky knees."*

JOB 4:4 NLT

God knows how weak and shaky we feel some days. He understands our feelings. After all, He made us, so He understands how prone humans are to discouragement. He doesn't blame us for being human, but He never leaves us helpless either. His grace is always there, like a hand held out to us, simply waiting for us to reach out and grasp it.

*Lord, thank You for Your words that give me support
and hope when I am falling; thank You for encouraging
me when I feel shaky. May I rest in Your
grace and truth. Amen.*

Day 84

TRUE BEAUTY

*What matters is not your outer appearance—the
styling of your hair, the jewelry you wear, the cut of your
clothes—but your inner disposition. Cultivate inner
beauty, the gentle, gracious kind that God delights in.*

1 PETER 3:3–4 MSG

We want to be beautiful. It's a longing that has been in
our hearts since we were little girls. As grown-up women,
we can become overly worried about our appearance,
fretting over whether we measure up to the demanding
standards of that little girl who still lives in our hearts.
We need to relax in the assurance of God's grace within
us. As we allow His Spirit to shine through us, we will
find our deepest, truest beauty.

*God, instead of focusing on the image I see in my
mirror, help me to look into Your eyes for an accurate
reflection of the beauty You have instilled in me. Amen.*

Day 85

OUR ROCK AND SAVIOR

"The LORD lives! Praise be to my Rock!
Exalted be my God, the Rock, my Savior!"
2 SAMUEL 22:47 NIV

Throughout the Psalms we read that David not only worshipped and praised God, but he also complained to Him, was honest with God about what he was feeling, and even admitted to being angry at God. Perhaps the most amazing thing about David, though, was his constant devotion and reliance on his Creator. Even though David is the powerful king of Israel, he praises God in 2 Samuel 22:47, calling Him his Rock and Savior. David knew God was alive, and he also knew he needed Him more than anything else in the world. It's the same for us today!

Dear Lord, You are my Rock and my Savior.
You are alive, and I praise You as God above all else.
Thank You for Your love and power. Amen.

Day 86

OUTSIDE OF TIME'S STREAM

Your throne, O LORD, has stood from time immemorial.
You yourself are from the everlasting past.

PSALM 93:2 NLT

If you think of time as a fast-moving river, then we are creatures caught in its stream. Life keeps slipping away from us like water between our fingers. But God is outside of time's stream. He holds our past safely in His hands, and His grace is permanent and unshakable. His love is the lifesaver to which we cling in the midst of time's wild waves.

God, when I try to understand words like immemorial
and everlasting, I am in awe. I cannot begin to
comprehend Your bigness. Give me Your
perspective. Help me to trust You. Amen.

Day 87

FIRST PRIORITIES

For Wisdom is better than all the trappings of wealth;
nothing you could wish for holds a candle to her.
PROVERBS 8:11 MSG

What do you value most? You may know the answer
you are "supposed" to give to that question, but you can
tell the real answer by where your time and energy are
focused. Do you spend most of your time working for
and thinking about money and physical wealth, or do
you make wisdom and grace your first priorities?

Father, if I compare myself too much with others,
I can easily get caught in the trappings of wealth.
Instead, turn my focus to You and help me
to make wisdom my goal. Amen.

Day 88

WHERE CREDIT IS DUE

*It is not that we think we are qualified to do anything
on our own. Our qualification comes from God.*
2 CORINTHIANS 3:5 NLT

It's easy to seek God when we feel like failures, but when
success comes our way, we like to congratulate ourselves
rather than give God the credit. When we achieve great
things, we need to remember that it is God's grace through
us that brought about our success.

*Father, every good thing I do comes from You.
Thank You for allowing me to collaborate with You to
do Your work. It is an honor to be used by You. Amen.*

Day 89

CONTROL

*Put God in charge of your work, then what
you've planned will take place.*
PROVERBS 16:3 MSG

If we're doing a job that is important to us, it is hard to let
go of our control. Not only do we hate to trust someone
else to take over, but we often don't want to trust God to
take charge either. We want to do it all by ourselves. But
the best-laid plans fall into nothing without God's help.
What's more, as we rely on His grace, we no longer need
to feel stressed or pressured! We can let Him take charge.

*God, the more I entrust my plans to You, the more
successful they will be. Give me the courage to trust
and the grace to rest in Your promise. Amen.*

Day 90

PLANTING

I planted the seed, Apollos watered it,
but God has been making it grow.

1 Corinthians 3:6 niv

Have you ever hesitated to engage in a spiritual discussion with a person because you didn't know how he would take it or you felt like you didn't have the time required to build a relationship with him? Of course, in an ideal world we'd have time to sit and chat with everyone for days, and the coffee would be free. But the fact that our world isn't ideal should not prevent us from planting a seed. You just never know what might happen to it. And that makes for some exciting gardening.

Dear God, thank You for allowing me to work for Your
kingdom. Help me to plant more seeds. Amen.

Day 91

WISE ENOUGH TO LEAD

"To God belong wisdom and power;
counsel and understanding are his."
JOB 12:13 NIV

The word *wisdom* comes from the same root words that have to do with vision, the ability to see into a deeper spiritual reality. Where else can we turn for the grace to see beneath life's surface except to God? Who else can we trust to be strong enough and wise enough to lead us to our eternal home?

Lord, my vision is far from 20/20. Help me see the world through Your lens of wisdom. Bestow on me Your counsel and fill me with Your understanding. Amen.

Day 92

HEARTFELT

For we live by believing and not by seeing.

2 CORINTHIANS 5:7 NLT

The world of science tells us that only what can be seen
and measured is truly real. But our hearts know differently.
Every day we depend on the things we believe—our faith
in God and in our friends and family, our commitment to
give ourselves to God and others—and it is these invisible
beliefs that give us grace to live.

*`Father, my mind is so prone to cling to what is tangible.
But my heart is sure that You are as real as the bright
shining sun. Fill me with confidence and trust. Amen.*

Day 93

A LOVELY PLACE

How lovely is your dwelling place, Lord Almighty!
PSALM 84:1 NIV

Imagine this: God considers your heart His home! It's the place where He dwells. And as a result, your heart is a lovely place, filled with the grace of the almighty God.

O Lord Almighty, I humbly invite You into my heart's home. Fill it with Your loveliness so I can experience the comfort of Your presence and Your peace. Amen.

Day 94

QUIET TIME

Rest in the LORD and wait patiently for Him.
PSALM 37:7 NASB

Our lives are busy. Responsibilities crowd our days, and at night as we go to bed, our minds often continue to be preoccupied with the day's work, ticking off a mental to-do list even as we fall asleep. We need to set aside time to quiet our hearts. In those moments we can let go of all our to-dos and wait for God's grace to take action in our lives.

God, thank You for this verse that reminds me of the gift of stillness. In my all-too-few quiet moments, help me learn to wait patiently for You. Amen.

Day 95

TRUTH

*"You will know the truth,
and the truth will set you free."*
JOHN 8:32 NLT

What lies do you believe about yourself? How might those lies be preventing you from experiencing God's plan for *your* life? The next time you're tempted to believe a lie, write it down. Then find a scripture passage that speaks truth over the situation. Write that scripture across the lie. Commit the truth to memory. Over time God's Word will transform your thinking, and you'll begin to believe the truth. Then something amazing will happen—you'll be set free.

*Father, thank You for the truth Your Word speaks
about my life. Open my eyes to the truth
and help me to believe it. Amen.*

Day 96

SEE JESUS

God left nothing that is not subject to them.
Yet at present we do not see everything
subject to them. But we do see Jesus.
HEBREWS 2:8–9 NIV

We know that Jesus has won the victory over sin, and yet when we look at the world as it is right now, we still see sin all around us. We see pain and suffering, greed and selfishness, brokenness and despair. We know the world is not ruled by God. Yet despite that, we can look past the darkness of sin. By grace, right now, we can see Jesus.

Jesus, when I am overwhelmed by the evil that seems to be winning in this world, remind me that You have won the victory. Give me the grace to see You. Amen.

Day 97

PEACE RULES

*And let the peace that comes from Christ rule
in your hearts. For as members of one
body you are called to live in peace.*
COLOSSIANS 3:15 NLT

Peace is a way of living our lives. It happens when we let Christ's peace into our lives to rule over our emotions, our doubts, and our worries, and then go one step more and let His peace control the way we live. Peace is God's gift of grace to us, but it is also the way to a graceful life, the path to harmony with the world around us.

*Jesus, what an amazing gift of peace that comes
from You. Thank You for leading me on
the path of a graceful life. Amen.*

Day 98

CAREFUL PLANS

Without good advice everything goes wrong—
it takes careful planning for things to go right.
PROVERBS 15:22 CEV

The Bible reminds us that when we start a new venture, we should not trust success to come automatically. We need to seek out the advice of those we trust. We need to make careful plans. And most of all, we need to seek God's counsel, praying for the grace and wisdom to do things right.

Father, there are so many opportunities for me
to grab hold of. It's tempting to dive in headfirst.
I desperately need Your counsel. Fill me
with Your grace and wisdom. Amen.

Day 99

MOVE ON

Anyone who belongs to Christ has become a new person. The old life is gone; a new life has begun!

2 Corinthians 5:17 nlt

You are a brand-new person in Jesus! Don't worry about what came before. Don't linger over your guilt and regret. Move on. Step out into the new, grace-filled life Christ has given you.

Heavenly Father, how grateful I am for new life! Thank You for putting to death the old me and for giving me the promise of a new life in Christ. Amen.

Day 100

CHRIST IS RISEN TODAY!

"He isn't here! He is risen from the dead!"
LUKE 24:6 NLT

The power God used to raise Christ from the dead is the same power we have available to us each day to live according to God's will here on earth. What happened on Easter gives us hope for today and for all eternity. If you haven't accepted Jesus Christ as your personal Savior, take the time right now and start your new life in Christ.

Dear Jesus, thank You for dying on the cross for me and taking away all my sin. You are alive and well, and I praise You today for all You are and all You have done. Amen.

Day 101

AMAZING EXPECTATIONS

*Listen to my voice in the morning, Lord. Each morning
I bring my requests to you and wait expectantly.*
PSALM 5:3 NLT

You need to get in the habit of hoping. Instead of getting
up in the morning and sighing as you face another dreary
day, practice saying hello to God as soon as you wake
up. Listen for what He wants to say to your heart. Expect
Him to do amazing things each day.

*Good morning, Lord. I can easily forget how necessary
it is to begin my day in sweet communion with
You. Tune my heart's ear to the lovely
sound of Your voice. Amen.*

Day 102

TRUTHS

For the word of God is alive and powerful. It is sharper than the sharpest two-edged sword, cutting between soul and spirit, between joint and marrow. It exposes our innermost thoughts and desires.

HEBREWS 4:12 NLT

God's words are not merely letters on a page. They are living things that work their way into our hearts and minds, revealing the fears and hopes we've kept hidden away, sometimes even from ourselves. Like a doctor's scalpel that cuts in order to heal, God's Word slices through our carefully created facades and exposes our deepest truths.

Father, how grateful I am for Your Word. I am amazed at the way it teaches me and exposes my true intentions. Help me to bravely submit myself to Your healing. Amen.

Day 103

UNFAILING LOVE

But I trust in your unfailing love.
I will rejoice because you have rescued me.
PSALM 13:5 NLT

Have you ever done that exercise in trust where you fall backward into another person's arms? It's hard to let yourself drop, trusting that the other person will catch you. The decision to let yourself fall is not an emotion that sweeps over you. It's just something you have to do, despite your fear. In the same way, we commit ourselves to God's unfailing love, finding new joy each time His arms keep us from falling.

Father, You have shown me time and time again
that I can trust You because You have consistently
rescued me with Your unfailing love.
I commit myself to Your loving arms. Amen.

Day 104

QUIET, GENTLE GRACE

"Let me teach you, because I am humble and gentle at heart, and you will find rest for your souls."

MATTHEW 11:29 NLT

Sometimes we keep trying to do things on our own, even though we don't know what we're doing and even though we're exhausted. And all the while, Jesus waits quietly, ready to show us the way. He will lead us with quiet, gentle grace, carrying our burdens for us. We don't have to try so hard. We can finally rest.

Jesus, I don't like feeling incompetent and inadequate. It makes me feel anxious and exhausted. Thank You for Your gentle teaching and for the strength You provide. Give me Your rest. Amen.

Day 105

FAITH AND ACTION

*And I keep praying that this faith we hold in
common keeps showing up in the good things we do,
and that people recognize Christ in all of it.*
PHILEMON 6 MSG

Our actions and reactions are a powerful gauge of how
serious we are about our faith. When others wrong us,
do we refuse to forgive and risk misrepresenting Christ,
or do we freely offer forgiveness as an expression of our
faith? God calls us to faith and forgiveness in Christ
Jesus so that Christians and non-Christians alike will
see our good deeds and praise God.

*Dear Lord, please let me remember that people
look to me for a glimpse of You. Let my actions
always reflect my faith in You. Amen.*

Day 106

FREE!

*For the Lord is the Spirit, and wherever
the Spirit of the Lord is, there is freedom.*

2 CORINTHIANS 3:17 NLT

How do you know when the Holy Spirit is present in your life? You should be able to tell by the sense of freedom you feel. If you feel oppressed, obsessed, or depressed, something in your life is out of kilter. Seek out God's Spirit. He wants you to be free.

*Holy Spirit, fill me with a sense of freedom only
You can provide. Free my spirit from chains of
oppression, and draw me into the wide
open spaces of Your peace. Amen.*

Day 107

BLESSING OTHERS

"Bless those who curse you.
Pray for those who hurt you."
LUKE 6:28 NLT

Not only does God bless us, but we are called to bless others. God wants to show the world His grace through us. He can do this when we show our commitment to make God's love real in the world around us through our words and actions, as well as through our prayer life. We offer blessings to others when we greet a scowl with a smile, when we refuse to respond to angry words, and when we offer understanding to those who are angry and hurt.

God, I sometimes forget that the world is watching.
I long to shine Your light to everyone I see.
Help me to bestow blessings on others,
even when they hurt me. Amen.

Day 108

BOARD GOD'S BOAT

Then, because so many people were coming and
going that they did not even have a chance to eat,
he said to them, "Come with me by yourselves
to a quiet place and get some rest."

MARK 6:31 NIV

The apostles ministered tirelessly—so much so, they had
little time to eat. As they gathered around Jesus to report
their activities, the Lord noticed they had neglected to take
time for themselves. Sensitive to their needs, the Savior
instructed them to retreat by boat with Him to a solitary
place of rest where He was able to minister to them.

Often we allow the hectic pace of daily life to drain
us physically and spiritually, and in the process, we
deny ourselves time alone to pray and read God's Word.
Meanwhile, God patiently waits.

So perhaps it's time to board God's boat to a quieter
place and not jump ship!

Heavenly Father, in my hectic life I've neglected
time apart with You. Help me to spend time
in Your Word and in prayer. Amen.

Day 109

ANSWERED KNEE-MAIL

*The prayer of a righteous person
is powerful and effective.*
JAMES 5:16 NIV

The concept of the power of prayer is familiar, but sometimes we forget what it means. Prayer is a powerful tool for communicating with God, an opportunity to commune with the Creator of the universe. Prayer is not something to be taken lightly or used infrequently. Yet, in the rush of daily life, we often lose sight of God's presence. Instead of turning to Him for guidance and comfort, we depend on our own resources.

But prayer isn't just a way to seek protection and guidance; it's how we develop a deeper relationship with our heavenly Father. We can access this power anywhere. We don't need a Wi-Fi hot spot or a high-speed modem. We just need to look up. He's connected and waiting.

*Father, thank You for being at my side all
the time. Help me to turn to You instantly,
in need and in praise. Amen.*

Day 110

DO A LITTLE DANCE

Then Miriam. . .took a tambourine and led all the
women as they played their tambourines and danced.
EXODUS 15:20 NLT

Can you imagine the enormous celebration that broke
out among the children of Israel when God miraculously
saved them from Pharaoh's army? Even dignified
prophetess Miriam grabbed her tambourine and cut
loose with her girlfriends. Despite adverse circumstances,
she heard God's music and did His dance. Isn't that
our goal today? To hear God's music above the world's
cacophony and do His dance as we recognize everyday
miracles in our lives?

Make me aware of Your everyday miracles,
Father. Help me listen closely for Your
music so I can join in the dance. Amen.

Day 111

UNCONDITIONAL GRACE

A friend loves at all times.
PROVERBS 17:17 NASB

Friends are the people you can allow to see you at your worst. They're the ones who can see you without your makeup. . .or walk in when your house is a mess. . . or overhear you acting like a thirteen-year-old—and they'll still be your friends. They reveal to you God's unconditional grace.

Dear Lord, thank You for my friends and the joy
we share. Thank You for their love for me—
even on my worst days. Help me to be
a true and loving friend. Amen.

Day 112

QUIET GRACE

Patient persistence pierces through indifference;
gentle speech breaks down rigid defenses.
PROVERBS 25:15 MSG

When we're in the midst of an argument, we often become fixated on winning. We turn conflicts into power struggles, and we want to come out the victor. By sheer force, if necessary, we want to shape people to our will. But that is not the way God treats us. His grace is gentle and patient rather than loud and forceful. We need to follow His example and let His quiet grace speak through us in His timing rather than ours.

Father, thank You for the gentleness of Your grace.
Give me a spirit of patient persistence. Instill my
words with gentleness. May I always value
relationships over being right. Amen.

Day 113

NO LIMITS

Great is our Lord, and of great power:
his understanding is infinite.
PSALM 147:5 KJV

When you're praying for wisdom in a complex or desperate situation, fix this thought firmly in your mind: You may have no clue as to the right answer, but God certainly does! His understanding is without end.

At times, we don't understand why God allows us to go through troubled times, but He certainly knows—and He cares deeply for each one of us. He not only knows every star by name, but He knows *your* name too.

Psalm 147:5 is one of the most powerful scriptures in the Bible. When we meditate deeply on its words, they can fill our minds with peace and assurance.

God, who am I among all the stars in the universe?
But You know their names, and You know
mine too! You know me, You understand
me, and that brings me peace. Amen.

Day 114

THE VERY BEST

*"But if you remain in me and my words remain
in you, you may ask for anything you
want, and it will be granted!"*
JOHN 15:7 NLT

Wow! Really? Is that true?

As silly as this may sound, there are some who assume they have license to treat God as a concierge of some kind, who is standing by to rush to fulfill their every request.

As we present our requests to God, we need to realize that He knows what is best for us and that we should never demand "our way." We must not forget the first part of John 15:7 that says, "If you remain in me and my words remain in you." This should clearly tell us that our first desires need to be that God's will is done.

Since God only wants to give us the very best, and He knows how to make that happen, why would we pray for anything else?

*Father, I say, "Thy will be done!" You know best.
I want what You want for me, even if it's
not what I ask for. Amen.*

Day 115

NEVER LOST FOR LONG

For "whoever calls on the name
of the LORD shall be saved."
ROMANS 10:13 NKJV

You call out to God, but maybe for a little while you don't hear anything. You may have to listen intently for a while, but eventually you are reassured by His voice. When He calls your name, you know you are safe. You may have to take a few steps in the dark, but by moving toward Him, you eventually see clearly. A light comes on in your heart, and you recognize where you are and what you need to do to get back on the path God has set before you.

Heavenly Father, help me to stay focused on You.
Show me how to remove distractions from my
life so I can stay close to You. Amen.

Day 116

OUR COMPANION

Our Lord, you are the friend of your worshipers,
and you make an agreement with all of us.

PSALM 25:14 CEV

God is our Friend. He is our Companion through life's
journey; He is the One who always understands us; and
no matter what we do, He always accepts us and loves us.
What better agreement could we ever have with anyone
than what we have with God?

Father, thank You for being my Friend, my Companion,
my comfort. Thank You for the everlasting covenant
You have made with me. I am grateful
to be Your child. Amen.

Day 117

WHEN WORDS FAIL ME

Before a word is on my tongue you,
Lord, know it completely.
PSALM 139:4 NIV

Sometimes Christians feel so overwhelmed by their needs or by the greatness of God that they simply can't pray. When the words won't come, God helps to create them. Paul says in Romans 8:26 (NLT), "And the Holy Spirit helps us in our weakness. For example, we don't know what God wants us to pray for. But the Holy Spirit prays for us with groanings that cannot be expressed in words."

God hears your prayers even before you pray them. When you don't know what to say and the words won't come, you can simply ask God to help you by praying on your behalf.

Dear God, I'm grateful today that
in my silence You still hear me. Amen.

Day 118

CONSTANT GRACE

For Jesus doesn't change—yesterday, today,
tomorrow, he's always totally himself.
HEBREWS 13:8 MSG

As human beings, we live in the stream of time. Sometimes all the changes time brings terrify us; sometimes they fill us with joy and excitement. Either way, we can cling to the still point that lies in the middle of our changing world: Jesus Christ, who never changes. His constant grace leads us through all life's changes, and one day it will bring us to our home in heaven, beyond time, where we will be like Him.

Jesus, how grateful I am that You stay the same.
Yesterday, today, and forever, I can count on
You to remain firm and steadfast, no matter
how much change life brings. Amen.

Day 119

NEW STRENGTH

"In quietness and confidence is your strength."
ISAIAH 30:15 NLT

The weaker we feel, the more we fret. The more we fret, the weaker we feel. It's a vicious circle. Stop the circle! Find a quiet place, if only for a few moments, to draw close to God. Grace will come to you through the quiet, and you will discover new strength.

Father, I desperately need You. Step in and take me out of the vicious circle of worry and fretting. Give me Your peace. Thank You for Your strength. Amen.

Day 120

OUR SONG

*By day the LORD directs his love, at night his song
is with me—a prayer to the God of my life.*

PSALM 42:8 NIV

All through the Bible, we find people worshipping God
through song. They sing to God about winning battles and
the birth of babies. They sing songs of lament and songs
of praise, songs sinking with sorrow and songs bouncing
with joy. There is, of course, a whole book devoted just
to this exercise: Psalms. . . . By day God guides us, and at
night He still leaves the doors of communication open.
What do you think His song is saying to you? What do
you want to sing to Him?

*Dear God, help me listen for Your song and help me
find the words to sing praise to You every day. Amen.*

Day 121

SIMPLY HAPPY

Are any of you happy? You should sing praises.
JAMES 5:13 NLT

Some days are simply happy days. The sun shines, people make us laugh, and life seems good. A day like that is a special grace. Thank God for it. As you hum through your day, don't forget to sing His praises.

Father, thank You for the gift of happiness and for life in the Holy Spirit that allows me to sing praises through my days. I praise You with all my heart. Amen.

Day 122

YOUNG

Honor and enjoy your Creator
while you're still young.
ECCLESIASTES 12:1 MSG

Young is a matter of perspective. Some people are old at fifteen, and others are still young at ninety. As we enjoy the God who made us, honoring Him in all we do, His grace will keep us young.

Father, my Creator, instill within my spirit a longing
to honor You and enjoy You all the days of my
life. May Your grace continue to amaze
me and keep me young. Amen.

Day 123

ONLY BY GRACE

Accept one another, then, just as Christ accepted you, in order to bring praise to God.
ROMANS 15:7 NIV

It's easy to pick out others' faults. Sometimes you may even feel justified in doing so, as though God will approve of your righteousness as you point out others' sinfulness. Don't forget that Christ accepted you, with all your brokenness and faults. Only by grace were you made whole. Share that grace—that acceptance and unconditional love—with the people around you.

Jesus, what a joy it is to know that You have accepted me just as I am! You have made me whole. Help me to pass that grace on to others. Amen.

Day 124

ON TRUTH'S SIDE

We're rooting for the truth to win out in you.
We couldn't possibly do otherwise.

2 Corinthians 13:8 msg

As we look at the world around us, we can see that people often prefer falsehoods to truth. They choose to live in a world that soothes their anxiety, rather than face life's reality. We cannot force people to acknowledge what they don't want to face, but we can do all we can to encourage them and build them up. We can cheer for the truth, trusting that God's grace is always on truth's side.

Father, Author of truth, open my eyes to the truth
of Your Word. Help me not to be swayed by
falsehood but instead cling to Your truth. Amen.

Day 125

A VALUABLE DEPOSIT

He anointed us, set his seal of ownership on us,
and put his Spirit in our hearts as a deposit,
guaranteeing what is to come.

2 CORINTHIANS 1:21–22 NIV

When we commit our lives to Christ, He doesn't let us flail around in this mixed-up world without any help. We have the deposit of the Holy Spirit with us all the time, and He also gives us His Word and the help of other Christians to keep us strong in the Lord. So whenever you feel alone or overwhelmed with life, remember that God has anointed you, set His seal upon you, and deposited the Holy Spirit right inside your heart. That is the most valuable deposit of all!

Dear Lord, thank You for depositing Your
Holy Spirit in my heart to lead and guide
me. Help me to listen. Amen.

Day 126

SENSITIVITY

*At the same time, don't be callous in your exercise
of freedom, thoughtlessly stepping on the toes of
those who aren't as free as you are. I try my best
to be considerate of everyone's feelings in all
these matters; I hope you will be, too.*

1 Corinthians 10:32–33 MSG

The person who walks in grace doesn't trip over other
people's feet. She doesn't shove her way through life like
a bull in a china shop. Instead, she allows the grace she
has so freely received to make her more aware of others'
feelings. With God-given empathy, she is sensitive to
those around her, sharing the grace she has received
with all she meets.

*Jesus, I am grateful for the freedom I have in You.
Help me to see past my differences with others
so that I can show them empathy from a
gracious and compassionate heart. Amen.*

Day 127

TRUE NOURISHMENT

He gives food to every living thing.
His faithful love endures forever.
PSALM 136:25 NLT

People often have a confused relationship with food. We love to eat, but we feel guilty when we do. We sometimes turn to food when we're tense or worried, trying to fill the empty, anxious holes in our hearts. But God wants to give us the true nourishment we need, body and soul, if only we will let Him.

Heavenly Father, any of Your good gifts used for the wrong reasons or in excess have the potential to harm me. Help me to have a healthy relationship with food. Amen.

Day 128

WHAT YOU CRAVE

Take delight in the Lord, and he will
give you your heart's desires.

PSALM 37:4 NLT

Do you ever feel as though God wants to deny you what you want, as though He's a cruel stepparent who takes pleasure in thwarting you? That image of God is a lie. He's the One who placed your heart's desires deep inside you. As you turn to Him, knowing He alone is the source of all true delight, He will grant you what your heart most truly craves.

Father, I cannot imagine that You love me so much that
You would reach out and give me the things my heart
desires. Yet Your Word is truth. Thank You. Amen.

Day 129

"EXTENDED" FAMILY

God sets the lonely in families.
PSALM 68:6 NIV

God knows we need others. We need their love and support, their understanding, and their simple physical presence nearby. That is why He gives us families. Families don't need to be related by blood, though. They might be the people you work with or the people you go to church with or the group of friends you've known since grade school. Whoever they are, they're the people who make God's grace real to you every day.

Father, thank You for creating me with a longing for connection. Thank You for those You have placed in my life to make me more of who You created me to be. Amen.

Day 130

PRAYER

*Jesus often withdrew to lonely
places and prayed.*
LUKE 5:16 NIV

Jesus is our perfect role model. If He withdrew often to pray, shouldn't we? Do we think we can continually give to others without getting replenished ourselves? Make prayer a priority. Recognize that the Lord must daily fill your cup so you will have something to give. Set aside a specific time, a specific place. Start slow. Give Him five minutes every day. As you are faithful, your relationship with Him will grow. Over time you will crave the time spent together as He fills your cup to overflowing. Follow Jesus' example and pray!

*Dear Lord, help me set aside time to pray each
day. Please fill my cup so I can share with
others what You have given me. Amen.*

Day 131

MOST IMPORTANT

Tune your ears to the world of Wisdom;
set your heart on a life of Understanding.

PROVERBS 2:2 MSG

What do you listen to most? Do you hear the world's voice, telling you to buy, buy, buy, to dress and look a certain way, to focus on things that won't last? Or have you tuned your ears to hear the quiet voice of God's wisdom? You can tell the answer to that question by your response to yet another question: What is most important to you? Things? Or the intangible grace of true understanding?

Lord, You are Wisdom. Tune my heart to Your wise
voice. Make Your priorities my priorities, and fill
my heart with Your wisdom and Your
understanding. Amen.

Day 132

GOD'S HONOR

For the honor of your name, O LORD,
forgive my many, many sins.
PSALM 25:11 NLT

Like all gifts of grace, forgiveness by its very definition is something that can never be earned. Forgiveness is what God gives us when we deserve nothing but anger. He forgives us not because we merit it but because of His own honor. Over and over we will turn away from God—but over and over He will bring us back. That is who He is!

Father, I am grateful for Your unending gift of
forgiveness. Help me relish in the joy of knowing
You always have and always will continue
to forgive my many sins. Amen.

Day 133

FOR ETERNITY

My health may fail, and my spirit may grow
weak, but God remains the strength
of my heart; he is mine forever.
PSALM 73:26 NLT

Sooner or later, our bodies let us down. Even the healthiest of us will one day have to face old age. When our bodies' strength fails us, we may feel discouraged and depressed. But even then we can find joy and strength in our God. When our hearts belong to the Creator of the universe, we realize we are far more than our bodies. Because of God's unfailing grace, we will be truly healthy for all eternity.

God, when I feel discouraged by aches and pains that
bring me down, help me remember that my life here on
earth is barely a breath in the scope of eternity. Amen.

Day 134

CHOOSE GRACE

*And a servant of the Lord must not quarrel but must
be kind to everyone, a good teacher, and patient.*

2 TIMOTHY 2:24 NCV

Some days we can't help but feel irritated and out of sorts.
But no matter how we feel on the inside, we can choose
our outward behavior. We can make the decision to let
disagreements go, to refuse to argue, to act in kindness,
to show patience and a willingness to listen (even when
we feel impatient). We can choose to walk in grace.

*Lord, help me be kind to everyone, to be a good teacher,
and to be patient with others. Thank You for Your
grace that allows me to be Your servant. Amen.*

Day 135

FEAR AND DREAD

"What I feared has come upon me;
what I dreaded has happened to me."
JOB 3:25 NIV

Do you have a secret fear or dread? God knew Job's secret fears but still called him "blameless and upright" (Job 1:8 NIV). God doesn't withhold His love if we harbor unspoken dread. He doesn't love us any less because of secret anxieties. The Lord "is like a father to his children. . . . He remembers we are only dust" (Psalm 103:13–14 NLT). God never condemned Job (and He'll never condemn us) for private fears. He encourages us, as He did Job, to trust Him. He alone retains control over all creation and all circumstances (Job 38–41).

Father, please stay beside me when what
I dread most comes to me. Amen.

Day 136

WITNESS OF LAUGHTER

We were filled with laughter, and we sang for joy.
And the other nations said, "What amazing
things the LORD has done for them."

PSALM 126:2 NLT

Life is truly amazing. Each day, grace touches us in many ways, from the sun on our faces to each person we meet, from the love of our friends and families to the satisfaction of our work. Pay attention. Let people hear you laugh more. Don't hide your joy. It's a witness to God's love.

Father, thank You for this amazing life and for Your
grace that touches me in so many ways. Help me
to wear my joy for all to see. Amen.

Day 137

SIMPLY LOVE

But I am giving you a new command.
You must love each other, just as I have loved you.
JOHN 13:34 CEV

Christ doesn't ask us to point out others' faults. He doesn't require that we be the morality squad, focusing on all that is sinful in the world around us. Instead, He wants us simply to love, just as He loves us. When we do, the world will see God's grace shining in our lives.

Jesus, there is such simplicity in merely loving
others with Your love. Help me to follow this
new command and let the world see
Your grace shining in my life. Amen.

Day 138

NOTHING MORE VALUABLE

*"Wisdom is more valuable than gold
and crystal. It cannot be purchased
with jewels mounted in fine gold."*

JOB 28:17 NLT

Money can't buy you love—and it can't buy wisdom either. Wisdom is more precious than anything this world has to offer. In fact, some passages of the Old Testament seem to indicate that Wisdom is another name for Jesus. Just as Jesus is the Way, the Truth, and the Life, He is also the One who gives us the vision to see God's world all around us. No other gift is more valuable than Jesus.

*Jesus, the Way, the Truth, and the Life, give me
Your vision. Help me see the world through
Your eyes. Help me place my relationship
with You above all else. Amen.*

Day 139

DRAWING BACK THE CURTAINS

*But whenever someone turns to the Lord, the veil is
taken away.... So all of us who have had that veil
removed can see and reflect the glory of the Lord.
And the Lord—who is the Spirit—makes
us more and more like him as we are
changed into his glorious image.*

2 CORINTHIANS 3:16, 18 NLT

Sometimes we feel as though a thick, dark curtain hangs
between us and God, hiding Him from our sight. But the
Bible says that all we have to do is turn our hearts to the
Lord and the curtain will be drawn back, letting God's
glory and grace shine into our lives. When that happens,
we can soak up the light, allowing it to renew our hearts
and minds into the image of Christ.

*Lord, thank You for removing the veil that hung
between us. Turn my heart to You and draw me to
Your light, renewing my heart and mind and
making me more like Christ. Amen.*

Day 140

HOLD HIS HAND

"For I am the LORD your God who takes hold of your right hand and says to you, Do not fear; I will help you."

ISAIAH 41:13 NIV

God desires to help us. When we walk through life hand in hand with God, we can face anything. His love covers us. His presence is our guard. We can do all things through Christ because we are given His strength. Do you feel as though you're walking through life alone? Do not fear. Are you in need of love, protection, courage, and strength? Reach out your hand. Allow Jesus to take hold of it. Receive His love and protection. Bask in His courage and strength. Take hold of His hand!

Dear Lord, thank You that I do not have to fear. You will help me by taking my hand. Amen.

Day 141

YOUR BEST FRIEND

*God is faithful, who has called you into fellowship
with his Son, Jesus Christ our Lord.*
1 CORINTHIANS 1:9 NIV

When do you pray? How often do you call on God? Where do you talk to Him?

When, where, or how we talk to God is of little importance to the Savior. We can converse with the Lord while driving down the street, walking through the park, or standing at the kitchen sink. We can ask for His help with the most insignificant or even the biggest decisions. Our concerns are His concerns too, and He desires for us to share our heartfelt thoughts with Him.

Fellowshipping with God is talking to our best Friend, knowing He understands and provides help and wisdom along life's journey. It's demonstrating our faith and trust in the One who knows us better than anyone.

*Lord, remind me to talk to You anytime, anywhere.
I know that as I pray You will talk to me too. Amen.*

Day 142

THE SECRET OF SERENDIPITY

A happy heart makes the face cheerful.
PROVERBS 15:13 NIV

Can you remember the last time you laughed in wild abandon? Better yet, when was the last time you did something fun, outrageous, or out of the ordinary? Perhaps it is an activity you haven't done since you were a child, like slip down a waterslide, strap on a pair of ice skates, or pitch a tent and camp overnight. A happy heart turns life's situations into opportunities for fun. When we seek innocent pleasures, we glean the benefits of a happy heart. So try a bit of whimsy just for fun. And rediscover the secret of serendipity.

Dear Lord, because of You, I have a happy
heart. Lead me to do something fun
and spontaneous today! Amen.

Day 143

PUT ON A HAPPY FACE

*He restoreth my soul: he leadeth me in the paths
of righteousness for his name's sake.*

PSALM 23:3 KJV

Our God is not a God of negativity but of possibility. He
will guide us through our difficulties and beyond them.
Today we should turn our thoughts and prayers toward
Him. Focus on a hymn or a praise song and play it in your
mind. Praise chases away the doldrums and tips our lips
up in a smile. With a renewed spirit of optimism and hope
we can thank the Giver of all things good. Thankfulness
to the Father can turn our plastic smiles into real ones,
and, as the psalm states, our souls will be restored.

*Father, I'm down in the dumps today. You are my
unending source of strength. Gather me
in Your arms for always. Amen.*

Day 144

ANSWER ME, GOD!

Answer me when I call to you, my righteous God.
Give me relief from my distress; have mercy
on me and hear my prayer.

PSALM 4:1 NIV

No matter our maturity level, there will be times when we feel abandoned by God. There will be times when our faith wavers and our fortitude wanes. That's okay. It's normal.

But David didn't give up. He kept crying out to God, kept falling to his knees in worship, kept storming God's presence with his pleas. David knew God wouldn't hide His face for long, for he knew what we might sometimes forget: God is love. He loves us without condition and without limit. And He is never far from those He loves.

No matter how distant God may seem, we need to keep talking to Him. Keep praying. Keep pouring out our hearts. We can know, as David knew, that God will answer in His time.

Dear Father, thank You for always hearing my
prayers. Help me to trust You, even when
You seem distant. Amen.

Day 145

MY FUTURE IS IN YOUR HANDS

*The Lord says, "I will guide you along the best pathway
for your life. I will advise you and watch over you."*
PSALM 32:8 NLT

Are plans running wild in your head? Remember that
the Lord is watching over you, and He is there to guide
you. He wants you to seek Him out. Don't try to make
your dreams happen all by yourself. Get on your knees
and ask Him to direct your plans each morning. Don't
be afraid to put your future in His hands!

*Father, thank You for always being faithful to me.
Continue to watch over me and direct my path. Amen.*

Day 146

LIFE PRESERVERS

My comfort in my suffering is this:
Your promise preserves my life.

PSALM 119:50 NIV

In the difficulties of life, God is our life preserver. When we are battered by the waves of trouble, we can expect God to understand and to comfort us in our distress. His Word, like a buoyant life preserver, holds us up in the bad times. But the life preserver only works if you put it on *before* your boat sinks. God will surround you with His love and protection—even if you're unconscious of His presence. He promises to keep our heads above water in the storms of living.

Preserving God, I cling to You as my life preserver.
Keep my head above the turbulent waters so I don't
drown. Bring me safely to the shore. Amen.

Day 147

REJOICING WITH FRIENDS

*"Then he calls his friends and neighbors together and
says, 'Rejoice with me; I have found my lost sheep.'"*
LUKE 15:6 NIV

Think of all the reasons you have to celebrate. Are you in
good health? Have you overcome a tough obstacle? Are
you handling your finances without much grief? Doing
well at your job? Bonding with friends or family? If so,
then throw yourself a party and invite a friend. Better yet,
call your friends and neighbors together, as the scripture
indicates. Share your praises with people who will truly
appreciate all that the Lord is doing in your life. Let the
party begin!

*Lord, thank You that I'm created in the image of a God
who knows how to celebrate. I have so many reasons
to rejoice today. Thank You for Your many blessings.
And today I especially want to thank You for giving
me friends to share my joys and sorrows. Amen.*

Day 148

MIRROR IMAGE

Behold, thou art fair, my love; behold,
thou art fair; thou hast doves' eyes.
SONG OF SOLOMON 1:15 KJV

No matter how hard we try, when the focus is on self, we see shortcomings. Our only hope is to see ourselves through a different mirror. We must remember that as we grow as Christians we take on the characteristics of Christ. The more we become like Him, the more beautiful we are in our own eyes and to those around us. God loves to behold us when we are covered in Christ. The mirror image He sees has none of the blemishes or imperfections, only the beauty.

O God, thank You for beholding me as being
fair and valuable. Help me to see myself
through Your eyes. Amen.

Day 149

WHY ME?

*I am Alpha and Omega, the beginning and the
ending, saith the Lord, which is, and which
was, and which is to come, the Almighty.*
REVELATION 1:8 KJV

When God spoke our world into existence, He called
into being a certain reality, knowing then everything
that ever was to happen—and everyone who ever was to
be. That you exist now is cause for rejoicing! God made
you to fellowship with Him! If that fellowship demands
trials for a season, rejoice that God thinks you worthy to
share in the sufferings of Christ—and, eventually, in His
glory. Praise His holy name!

*Father, I thank You for giving me this difficult time
in my life. Shine through all my trials today.
I want You to get the glory. Amen.*

Day 150

LEARN CONTENTMENT

*I am not saying this because I am in need, for I have
learned to be content whatever the circumstances.*

PHILIPPIANS 4:11 NIV

Contentment is learned and cultivated. It is an attitude of
the heart. It has nothing to do with material possessions
or life's circumstances. It has everything to do with being
in the center of God's will and knowing it. Contentment
means finding rest and peace in God's presence—nothing
more, nothing less. It is trusting that God will meet all
of your needs. May we learn to say confidently, *The Lord
is my Shepherd, I shall not want.* That is the secret of
contentment.

*Dear Lord, teach me how to be content in You,
knowing You will provide all that I need. Amen.*

Day 151

PROMISES OF GOD

"For the LORD your God is living among you.
He is a mighty savior. He will take delight in you
with gladness. With his love, he will calm all your
fears. He will rejoice over you with joyful songs."
ZEPHANIAH 3:17 NLT

Look at all the promises packed into this one verse of scripture! God is with you. He is your mighty Savior. He delights in you with gladness. He calms your fears with His love. He rejoices over you with joyful songs. Wow! What a bundle of hope is found here for the believer. Like a mother attuned to her newborn baby's cries, so is your heavenly Father's heart for you. He delights in being your Father. You are blessed to be a daughter of the King.

Father, thank You for loving me the way
You do. You are all I need. Amen.

Day 152

RADIANT

"If you are filled with light, with no dark corners,
then your whole life will be radiant, as though
a floodlight were filling you with light."

LUKE 11:36 NLT

We all have dark corners in our lives that we keep hidden. We hide them from others. We hide them from God, and we even try to hide them from ourselves. But God wants to shine His light even into our darkest, most private nooks and crannies. He wants us to step out into the floodlight of His love—and then His grace will make us shine.

Heavenly Father, fill me with light. Shine Your radiance on all my dark corners. Remove my shame and help me to bask in the light of Your love. Amen.

Day 153

STOP AND CONSIDER

"Listen to this, Job; stop and consider God's wonders.
Do you know how God controls the clouds and makes
his lightning flash? Do you know how the clouds
hang poised, those wonders of him who
has perfect knowledge?"

JOB 37:14–16 NIV

"Stop and consider My wonders," God told Job. Then He pointed to ordinary observations of the natural world surrounding Job—the clouds that hung poised in the sky, the flashes of lightning. "Not so very ordinary" was God's lesson. Maybe He was trying to remind us there is no such thing as ordinary. Let's open our eyes and see the wonders around us.

O Father, teach me to stop and consider the ordinary
moments of my life as reminders of You. Help me not
to overlook Your daily care and provisions
that surround my day. Amen.

Day 154

FAITH, THE EMOTIONAL BALANCER

No man is justified by the law in the sight of God,
it is evident: for, The just shall live by faith.
GALATIANS 3:11 KJV

Emotions mislead us. One day shines with promise as we bounce out of bed in song, while the next day dims in despair and we'd prefer to hide under the bedcovers. It has been said that faith is the bird that feels the light and sings to greet the dawn while it is still dark. The Bible instructs us to live by faith—not by feelings. Faith assures us that daylight will dawn in our darkest moments, affirming God's presence so that even when we fail to pray and positive feelings fade, our moods surrender to song.

Heavenly Father, I desire for my faith, not my
emotions, to dictate my life. I pray for balance
in my hide-under-the-covers days so that
I might surrender to You in song. Amen.

Day 155

HE IS FAITHFUL

If we are unfaithful, he remains faithful,
for he cannot deny who he is.

2 TIMOTHY 2:13 NLT

Sometimes we treat our relationship with God the same as we do with other people. We promise Him we'll start spending more time with Him in prayer and Bible study. Soon the daily distractions of life get in the way, and we're back in our same routine, minus prayer and Bible study.

Even when we fail to live up to our expectations, our heavenly Father doesn't pick up His judge's gavel and condemn us for unfaithfulness. Instead, He remains a faithful supporter, encouraging us to keep trying to hold up our end of the bargain. Take comfort in His faithfulness, and let that encourage you toward a deeper relationship with Him.

Father, thank You for Your unending faithfulness.
Every day I fall short of Your standards, but You're
always there, encouraging me and lifting me up.
Please help me to be more faithful to You—
in the big things and in the little things. Amen.

Day 156

LOVE IS BIGGER

"Love the LORD your God with all your heart and with all your soul and with all your might."
DEUTERONOMY 6:5 NASB

Love is not merely a feeling. It's far bigger than that. Love fills up our emotions, but it also fills our thoughts. Our body's strength and energy feed it. It requires discipline and determination. Loving God requires the effort of our whole being.

O Lord, help me learn to love You with all my heart, all my soul, and all my might. Give me the discipline and determination I need to love You fiercely. Amen.

Day 157

THE RIGHT PEOPLE

The LORD God said, "It isn't good for the man to live alone. I need to make a suitable partner for him."
GENESIS 2:18 CEV

God understands that human beings need each other. His love comes to us through others. That is the way He designed us, and we can trust His grace to bring the right people along when we need them, the people who will banish our loneliness and share our lives.

God, thank You for creating me to live in harmony with other people. Thank You for showing me Your love through others. Help me to love them well. Amen.

Day 158

MARVELOUS PLANS

Lord, you are my God; I will exalt you and praise
your name, for in perfect faithfulness you have done
wonderful things, things planned long ago.

ISAIAH 25:1 NIV

God has a "promised land" for us all—a marvelous plan for
our lives. Recount and record His faithfulness in your life
in the past, because God has already demonstrated His
marvelous plans to you in so many ways. Then prayerfully
anticipate the future journey with Him. Keep a record of
God's marvelous plans in a journal as He unfolds them
day by day. You will find God to be faithful in the smallest
aspects of your life and oh-so-worthy of your trust.

O Lord, help me to recount Your faithfulness, record
Your faithfulness, and trust Your faithfulness in
the future. For You are my God, and You have done
marvelous things, planned long ago. Amen.

Day 159

CHOOSE LIFE

*"The thief comes only to steal and kill and
destroy; I have come that they may have life,
and have it to the full."*

JOHN 10:10 NIV

God's Word shows us the lie—and the "liar"—behind
defeating thoughts. We have an enemy who delights in
our believing negative things, an enemy who wants only
destruction for our souls. But Jesus came to give us life!
We only have to choose it, as an act of the will blended
with faith. When we rely on Him alone, He'll enable us
not only to survive but to *thrive* in our daily routine. Each
day, let's make a conscious decision to take hold of what
Christ offers us—life, to the full.

*Loving Lord, help me daily to choose You and the life
You want to give me. Give me the eyes of faith to trust
that You will enable me to serve lovingly. Amen.*

Day 160

HEAVENLY APPRECIATION

God is not unjust; he will not forget your work
and the love you have shown him as you have
helped his people and continue to help them.
HEBREWS 6:10 NIV

Sometimes it seems our hard work is ignored. When our work for Christ seems to go unnoticed by our church family, we can be assured that God sees our hard work and appreciates it. We may not receive the "church member of the month" award, but our love for our brothers and sisters in Christ and our work on their behalf is not overlooked by God. The author of Hebrews assures us that God is not unjust—our reward is in heaven.

Dear Lord, You are a God of love and justice.
Even when I do not receive the notice of those around
me, help me to serve You out of my love for You. Amen.

Day 161

A GIFT

Don't you see that children are GOD's best gift?
PSALM 127:3 MSG

Whether we have children of our own or enjoy others' children, God's grace is revealed to us in a special way through these small people. In children, we catch a glimpse of what God intended for us all, before we grew up and let life cloud our hearts. Children's hope gives us grown-ups hope as well. Their laughter makes us smile, and their love reminds us that we too are loved by God.

Father, thank You for the joy that children bring and the beautiful illustration of Your love for us. Thank You for the life lessons little ones have to teach us. Amen.

Day 162

PRACTICALITY VS. PASSION

Leaving her water jar, the woman went back to the town and said to the people, "Come, see a man who told me everything I ever did. Could this be the Messiah?"

JOHN 4:28–29 NIV

Practicality gave way to passion the day the woman at the well abandoned her task, laid down her jar, and ran into town. Everything changed the day she met a man at the well and He asked her for a drink of water. Although they had never met before, He told her everything she had ever done, and then He offered her living water that would never run dry. Do you live with such passion, or do you cling to your water jar? Has an encounter with Christ made an impact that cannot be denied in your life?

Lord, help me to lay down anything that stifles my passion for sharing the Good News with others. Amen.

Day 163

HAVE YOU LOOKED UP?

The heavens proclaim the glory of God. The skies display his craftsmanship. Day after day they continue to speak; night after night they make him known.
PSALM 19:1-2 NLT

God has placed glimpses of creation's majesty—evidence of His love—throughout our world. Sunsets, seashells, flowers, snowflakes, changing seasons, moonlit shadows. Such glories are right in front of us, every single day! But we must develop eyes to see these reminders in our daily life and not let the cares and busyness of our lives keep our heads turned down. Have you looked up today?

Lord, open my eyes! Unstuff my ears! Teach me to see the wonders of Your creation every day and to point them out to others. Amen.

Day 164

FOLLOW THE LORD'S FOOTSTEPS

Then He said to them, "Follow Me,
and I will make you fishers of men."
MATTHEW 4:19 NKJV

Jesus asked His disciples to follow Him, and He asks us to do the same. Following Jesus requires staying right on His heels. We need to be close enough to hear His whisper. Stay close to His heart by opening the Bible daily. Allow His Word to speak to your heart and give you direction. Throughout the day, offer up prayers for guidance and wisdom. Keep in step with Him, and His close presence will bless you beyond measure.

Dear Lord, grant me the desire to follow You.
Help me not to run ahead or lag behind. Amen.

Day 165

CHANGING OUR PERSPECTIVE

Turn my eyes away from worthless things;
preserve my life according to your word.
PSALM 119:37 NIV

The book of Psalms offers hundreds of verses that can easily become sentence prayers. "Turn my eyes away from worthless things" whispered before heading out to shop, turning on the television, or picking up a magazine can turn those experiences into opportunities to see God's hand at work in our lives. He can change our perspective. He will show us what has value for us. He can even change our appetites, causing us to desire the very things He wants for us. When we pray this prayer, we are asking God to show us what He wants for us. He knows us and loves us more than we know and love ourselves. We can trust His love and goodness to provide for our needs.

Father, imprint this scripture in my mind today.
In moments of need, help me remember to pray
this prayer and relinquish my desires to You.

Day 166

GROUNDED IN LOVE

*"You'll be built solid, grounded in righteousness,
far from any trouble—nothing to fear!"*
ISAIAH 54:14 MSG

Balance isn't something we can achieve in ourselves. Just when we think we have it all together, life has a tendency to come crashing down around our ears. But even in the midst of life's most chaotic moments, God gives us grace; He keeps us balanced in His love. Like a building that is built to sway in an earthquake without falling down, we will stay standing if we remain grounded in His love.

*Heavenly Father, keep me grounded in Your love.
Provide for me a strong foundation to keep me stable
through life's most chaotic moments. Thank You
for Your steady hand. Amen.*

Day 167

CHOSEN

*"Before I formed you in the womb I knew you
[and approved of you as My chosen instrument],
and before you were born I consecrated you."*

JEREMIAH 1:5 AMP

God said that before He formed Jeremiah in his
mother's womb, He knew him. God separated him
from everyone else to perform a specific task, and He
consecrated him for that purpose. We can be sure that
if God did that for Jeremiah, He did it for each one of
us. Nothing about us or our circumstances surprises
God. He knew about everything before we were born.
And He ordained that we should walk in those ways
because we are uniquely qualified by Him to do so.
What an awesome God we serve!

*Father, the thought that You chose me before the
foundation of the world and set me apart for a specific
calling is humbling. You are so good. May I go
forward with a renewed purpose in life. Amen.*

Day 168

MIND, BODY, SPIRIT. . .

I stretch myself out. I sleep.
Then I'm up again—rested, tall and steady.
PSALM 3:5 MSG

Rest is one of God's gifts to us, a gift we regularly need. In sleep, we are renewed, mind, body, and spirit. Don't turn away from this most natural and practical of gifts!

Father, the gift of sleep is a glorious thing.
Help me not to resist this gift, and help me to
recognize the necessity of being refreshed
and renewed by hours of rest. Amen.

Day 169

INFINITE AND PERSONAL

*Am I a God at hand, saith the L*ORD*, and not a God
afar off? . . . Do not I fill heaven and earth?*
JEREMIAH 23:23–24 KJV

God says that He is both close at hand and over all
there is. Whether your day is crumbling around you or
is the best day you have ever had, do you see God in it?
If the "sky is falling" or the sun is shining, do you still
recognize the One who orders all the planets and all
your days? Whether we see Him or not, God tells us He
is there. And He's here too—in the good times and bad.

*Lord, empower me to trust You when it's hard to
remember You are near. And help me to live
thankfully when times are good. Amen.*

Day 170

GOD AS HE REALLY IS

The Lord is compassionate and gracious, slow to anger,
abounding in love.... He does not treat us as our sins
deserve or repay us according to our iniquities.
PSALM 103:8, 10 NIV

Our attitude toward God can influence the way we handle what He has given us. Some people perceive God as a harsh and angry judge, impatiently tapping His foot, saying, "When will you ever get it right?" People who see God this way can become paralyzed by an unhealthy fear of Him. But the Bible paints a very different picture of God. Psalm 103 says He is gracious and compassionate, that He does not treat us as our sins deserve. What difference can it make in your life to know you serve a loving God who is longing to be gracious to you?

Lord, thank You for Your compassion, Your grace, and
Your mercy. Help me to see You as You really are.

Day 171

LAW OF LOVE

I pondered the direction of my life,
and I turned to follow your laws.
PSALM 119:59 NLT

Did you know that the word *law* comes from root words that mean "foundation" or "something firm and fixed"? Sometimes we can't help but feel confused and uncertain. When that happens, turn to God's law, His rule for living. Love is His law, the foundation that always holds firm. When we cling to that, we find direction.

Lord, when I ponder the direction of my life without
Your Spirit, I am lost and uncertain. Thank You
for Your Word that anchors me in truth and
provides the guidance I need. Amen.

Day 172

REFRESHING GIFT

For we have great joy and consolation in
your love, because the hearts of the saints
have been refreshed by you, brother.
PHILEMON 7 NKJV

Jesus always took the time for those who reached out to Him. In a crowd of people, He stopped to help a woman who touched Him. His quiet love extended to everyone who asked, whether verbally or with unspoken need. God brings people into our path who need our encouragement. We must consider those around us. Smile and thank the waiter, the cashier, the people who help in small ways. Cheering others can have the effect of an energizing drink of water so they will be able to finish the race with a smile.

Jesus, thank You for being an example of how to
encourage and refresh others. Help me see their
need and be willing to reach out. Amen.

Day 173

ANNUAL OR PERENNIAL?

They are like trees planted along the riverbank,
bearing fruit each season. Their leaves never
wither, and they prosper in all they do.
PSALM 1:3 NLT

Annuals or perennials? Each has its advantages. Annuals are inexpensive, provide instant gratification, and keep boredom from setting in. Perennials require an initial investment but, when properly tended, faithfully provide beauty year after year—long after the annuals have dried up and withered away. Perennials are designed for the long haul—not just short-term enjoyment, but long-term beauty. The application to our lives is twofold. First, be a perennial—long lasting, enduring, slow growing, steady, and faithful. Second, don't be discouraged by your inevitable dormant seasons. Tend to your soul, and it will reward you with years of lush blossoms.

Father, be the Gardener of my soul. Amen.

Day 174

GOD IN THE DETAILS

*"When we heard of it, our hearts melted in fear
and everyone's courage failed because of you,
for the Lord your God is God in heaven
above and on the earth below."*

JOSHUA 2:11 NIV

Sometimes when our lives seem to be under siege from
the demands of work, bills, family—whatever—finding the
work of God amid the strife can be difficult. Even though
we acknowledge His power, we may overlook the gentle
touches, the small ways in which He makes every day
a little easier. Just as the Lord cares for the tiniest bird
(Matthew 10:29–31), so He seeks to be a part of every
detail in your life. Look for Him there.

*Father God, I know You are by my side every day,
good or bad, and that You love and care for me.
Help me to see Your work in my life and in
the lives of my friends and family. Amen.*

Day 175

PRIORITIZE PRAYER

*"But we will devote ourselves to prayer
and to the ministry of the word."*

ACTS 6:4 NASB

As busy women, we've found out the hard way that we can't do everything. Heaven knows we've tried, but the truth has found us out: superwoman is a myth. So we must make priorities and focus on the most important. Prayer and God's Word should be our faith priorities. If we only do as much as we can do, then God will take over and do what only He can do. He's got our backs, girls!

*I know I can't do it all, God. I find comfort in
knowing that if I put my faith in You wholeheartedly,
You will always help me prioritize my
to-do list and get the R&R I need.*

Day 176

HOLDING THE LINE

*When I said, "My foot is slipping," your unfailing love,
Lord, supported me. When anxiety was great
within me, your consolation brought me joy.*
<small>PSALM 94:18–19 NIV</small>

Often we may feel that our feet are slipping in life. We lose our grip. Anxiety becomes a sleep robber, headache giver, and joy squelcher. Fear takes over our hearts. All we can think is, *Just get me out of here!* But we must remember who is anchoring our life. God's powerful grip secures us—even in the most difficult times. He comforts us with His loving presence that defies understanding. He provides wisdom to guide our steps through life's toughest challenges. We can rest assured that His support is steady, reliable, and motivated by His love for us.

*Jesus, my Rock and fortress, thank You that Your
strength is made available to me. Steady me with
the surety of Your love. Replace my anxiety
with peace and joy, reflecting a life that's
secured by the Almighty. Amen.*

Day 177

SEEKING AN OASIS

*He changes a wilderness into a pool of water
and a dry land into springs of water.*

PSALM 107:35 NASB

The wilderness of Israel is truly a barren wasteland—
nothing but rocks and parched sand stretching as far as
the distant horizon. The life-and-death contrast between
stark desert and pools of oasis water is startling. Our lives
can feel parched too. Colorless. Devoid of life. But God
has the power to transform desert lives into gurgling,
spring-of-water lives. Ask Him to bubble up springs of
hope within you today.

*When I am feeling parched, Jesus, I trust
You'll create a peaceful oasis in my soul.
Envelop my spirit in Your hope, Lord.*

Day 178

LIFTED UP

But those who trust in the LORD will find new strength.
They will soar high on wings like eagles. They will run
and not grow weary. They will walk and not faint.

ISAIAH 40:31 NLT

Do you ever have days when you ask yourself, "How much further can I go? How much longer can I keep going like this?" On days like that, you long to give up. You wish you could just run away from the world and hide. Trust God's grace to give you the strength you need, even then. Let Him lift you up on eagle's wings.

Heavenly Father, I place my trust in You. Thank You
for the promise that I will soar high on eagle's
wings. Give me rest for my weariness and
strength for the journey. Amen.

Day 179

FAULTLESS

*To him who is able to keep you from stumbling
and to present you before his glorious presence
without fault and with great joy. . .*

JUDE 24 NIV

Jesus loves us so much despite our shortcomings. He is
the One who can keep us from falling—who can present
us faultless before the Father. Because of this we can
have our joy restored no matter what. Whether we have
done wrong and denied it or have been falsely accused,
we can come into His presence to be restored and lifted
up. Let us keep our eyes on Him instead of on our need
to justify ourselves to God or others.

*Thank You, Jesus, for Your cleansing love and for
the joy we can find in Your presence. Amen.*

Day 180

A NEW TOMORROW

Rahab the harlot...Joshua spared...for she hid the messengers whom Joshua sent to spy out Jericho.
JOSHUA 6:25 NASB

Rahab was the unlikeliest of heroes: a prostitute who sold her body in the darkest shadows. Yet she was the very person God chose to fulfill His prophecy. How astoundingly freeing! Especially for those of us ashamed of our past. God loved Rahab for who she was—not what she did. Rahab is proof that God can and will use anyone for His higher purposes. Anyone. Even you and me.

When I feel absolutely useless, God, remind me of Rahab's story. If You could use Rahab for Your purposes, You can certainly use me!

Day 181

ANXIOUS ANTICIPATIONS

I am not saying this because I am in need, for I have
learned to be content whatever the circumstances.

PHILIPPIANS 4:11 NIV

Have you ever been so eager for the future that you forgot to be thankful for the present day?

Humans have a tendency to complain about the problems and irritations of life. It's much less natural to appreciate the good things we have—until they're gone. While it's fine to look forward to the future, let's remember to reflect on all of *today's* blessings—the large and the small—and appreciate all that we do have.

Thank You, Lord, for the beauty of today.
Please remind me when I become preoccupied
with the future and forget to enjoy the present. Amen.

Day 182

REFLECTING GOD IN OUR WORK

Whatever you do, work at it with all your heart,
as working for the Lord, not for human masters.

COLOSSIANS 3:23 NIV

As believers, we are God's children. No one is perfect, and for this there is grace. But we may be the only reflection of our heavenly Father that some will ever see. Our attitudes and actions on the job speak volumes to those around us. Although it may be tempting to do just enough to get by, we put forth our best effort when we remember we represent God to the world. A Christian's character on the job should be a positive reflection of the Lord.

Father, help me today to represent You well through my
work. I want to reflect Your love in all I do. Amen.

Day 183

HIDE AND SEEK

*"But you, are you seeking great things for yourself?
Do not seek them; for behold, I am going to bring
disaster on all flesh," declares the Lord.*

JEREMIAH 45:5 NASB

God warns us: *Don't seek great things.* The more we seek them, the more elusive they become. As soon as we think we have them in our grasp, they disappear. If we commit to more activities than we can realistically handle, the best result is that we can't follow through. Worse, we might make them our god. Jesus tells us what we should seek: the kingdom of God and His righteousness (Matthew 6:33). When we seek the right things, He'll give us every good and perfect gift (James 1:17). And that will be more than we can ask or dream.

*Lord, please teach me to seek not greatness
but You. May You be the all in all of my life. Amen.*

Day 184

WALK CONFIDENTLY

*"But blessed are those who trust in the Lord and have
made the Lord their hope and confidence."*

JEREMIAH 17:7 NLT

What gives you confidence? Is it your clothes. . .your
money. . .your skills? These are all good things, but they
are blessings from God, given to you through His grace.
When your hopes (in other words, your expectations for
the future) rest only in God, then you can walk confidently,
knowing He will never disappoint you.

*Lord, You are my hope and my confidence. I place all
my expectations for the future in You, knowing You will
never disappoint me. Thank You for Your love. Amen.*

Day 185

LAUGH A RAINBOW

*"When I see the rainbow in the clouds, I will
remember the eternal covenant between God
and every living creature on earth."*
GENESIS 9:16 NLT

Ever feel like a cloud is hanging over your head?
Sometimes the cloud darkens to the color of bruises, and
we're deluged with cold rain that seems to have no end.
When you're in the midst of one of life's thunderstorms,
tape this saying to your mirror: Cry a river, laugh a
rainbow. The rainbow, the symbol of hope God gave
Noah after the flood, reminds us even today that every
storm will eventually pass.

*The rainbows You place in the sky after a storm
are lovely reminders of the hope we have in You,
God. Because of You, I know the storms of life
are only temporary. . .and You will
bring beauty from the storms.*

Day 186

LOCATION, LOCATION, LOCATION

Those who live in the shelter of the Most High will find rest in the shadow of the Almighty. This I declare about the LORD: He alone is my refuge, my place of safety; he is my God, and I trust him.

PSALM 91:1–2 NLT

If something is getting you down in life, check your location. Where are your thoughts? Let what the world has conditioned you to think go in one ear and out the other. Stand on the truth, the promises of God's Word. Say of the Lord, "God is my refuge! I am hidden in Christ! Nothing can harm me. In Him I trust!" Say it loud. Say it often. Say it over and over until it becomes your reality. And you will find yourself dwelling in that secret place every moment of the day.

God, You are my refuge. When I abide in You, nothing can harm me. Your Word is the truth on which I rely. Fill me with Your light and the peace of Your love. It's You and me, Lord, all the way! Amen.

Day 187

BEAUTIFUL WORLD

"Walk out into the fields and look at the wildflowers."
MATTHEW 6:28 MSG

Take the time to go outdoors. Look at nature. You don't have to spend hours to realize how beautiful God made the world. A single flower, if you really look at it, could be enough to fill you with awe. Sometimes we only need something very simple to remind us of God's grace.

*Creator, Father, I am amazed by Your creation
and the goodness reflected in its beauty.
Help me take time to enjoy this gift, to be
filled to the brim with gratitude. Amen.*

Day 188

SIMPLY SILLY

A cheerful disposition is good for your health.
PROVERBS 17:22 MSG

Imagine the effect we could have on our world today if our countenance reflected the joy of the Lord all the time: at work, at home, at play. Jesus said, "I have told you this so that my joy may be in you and that your joy may be complete" (John 15:11 NIV). Is your cup of joy full? Have you laughed today? Not a small smile, but laughter. Maybe it's time we looked for something to laugh about and tasted joy. Jesus suggested it.

*Lord, help me find joy this day. Let me laugh
and give praises to the King. Amen.*

Day 189

JUST HALF A CUP

*"I am coming to you now, but I say these things while
I am still in the world, so that they may have
the full measure of my joy within them."*

JOHN 17:13 NIV

Our heavenly Father longs to bestow His richest blessings
and wisdom on us. He loves us, so He desires to fill our
cup to overflowing with the things He knows will bring
us pleasure and growth. Do you tell Him to stop pouring
when your cup is only half-full? You may not even realize
it, but perhaps your actions dictate that your cup remain
half-empty. Seek a full cup and enjoy the full measure of
the joy of the Lord.

*Dear Jesus, forgive me for not accepting the fullness
of Your blessings and Your joy. Help me see the ways
I prevent my cup from being filled to overflowing.
Thank You for wanting me to have the
fullness of Your joy. Amen.*

Day 190

GET ABOVE IT ALL

Set your minds and keep them set on what is above (the higher things), not on the things that are on the earth.
COLOSSIANS 3:2 AMPC

Sometimes the most difficult challenges you face play out in your head—where a struggle to control the outcome and work out the details of life can consume you. Once removed—far away from the details—you can see things from a higher perspective. Close your eyes and push out the thoughts that try to grab you and keep you tied to the things of the world. Reach out to God and let your spirit soar. Give your concerns to Him and let Him work out the details. Rest in Him and He'll carry you above it all, every step of the way.

God, You are far above any detail of life that concerns me. Help me trust You today for answers to those things that seem to bring me down. I purposefully set my heart and mind on You today.

Day 191

GRACE FOR EACH DAY

*May the Lord direct your hearts into God's
love and Christ's perseverance.*
2 Thessalonians 3:5 niv

Allow God to lead you each day. His grace will lead you deeper and deeper into the love of God—a love that heals your wounds and works through you to touch those around you. Just as Christ never gave up but let love lead Him all the way to the cross, so too God will direct you all the way, giving you the strength and the courage you need to face each challenge.

*Lord, direct my heart into Your love and into
the perseverance of Christ. Lead me, by Your
grace, into a deeper love for You. Amen.*

Day 192

RELEASE THE MUSIC WITHIN

*Those who are wise will find a time
and a way to do what is right.*
ECCLESIASTES 8:5 NLT

It has been said that many people go to their graves with their music still in them. Do you carry a song within your heart, waiting to be heard?

Whether we are eight or eighty, it is never too late to surrender our hopes and dreams to God. A wise woman trusts that God will help her find the time and manner in which to use her talents for His glory as she seeks His direction. Let the music begin.

*Dear Lord, my music is fading against the constant
beat of a busy pace. I surrender my gifts to You
and pray for the time and manner in which I
can use those gifts to touch my world. Amen.*

Day 193

POWER OF THE WORD

*"The Spirit gives life; the flesh counts for nothing.
The words I have spoken to you—they
are full of the Spirit and life."*

JOHN 6:63 NIV

Jesus told His followers that His words were Spirit and life. When we hear His Word, meditate on it, pray it, memorize it, and ask for faith to believe it, He comes to us in it and transforms our lives through it. Once the Word is in our minds or before our eyes and ears, the Holy Spirit can work it into our hearts and our consciences. Jesus told us to abide in His Word. . .putting ourselves in a place to hear and receive the Word. The rest is the beautiful and mysterious work of the Spirit.

*Thank You, Jesus, the Living Word, who changes
my heart and my mind through the
power of Your Word. Amen.*

Day 194

LIGHT MY PATH

Your word is a lamp for my feet, a light on my path.
PSALM 119:105 NIV

God's Word is like a streetlamp. Often we *think* we know where we're going and where the stumbling blocks are. We believe we can avoid pitfalls and maneuver the path successfully on our own. But the truth is that without God's Word we are walking in darkness, stumbling and tripping. When we sincerely begin to search God's Word, we find the path becomes clear. God's light allows us to live our lives in the most fulfilling way possible, a way planned out from the very beginning by God Himself.

Jesus, shine Your light upon my path. I have spent too long wandering through the darkness, looking for my way. As I search Your Word, I ask You to make it a lamp to my feet so I can avoid the pitfalls of the world and walk safely along the path You have created specifically for me. Amen.

Day 195

THINKING HABITS

And now, dear brothers and sisters, one final thing.
Fix your thoughts on what is true, and honorable,
and right, and pure, and lovely, and admirable.
Think about things that are excellent
and worthy of praise.

PHILIPPIANS 4:8 NLT

Our brains are gifts from God, intended to serve us well, special gifts of grace we often take for granted. In return, we need to offer our minds back to God. Practice thinking positive thoughts. Focus on what is true rather than on lies; pay attention to beautiful things and stop staring at the ugly things in life. Discipline your mind to take on God's habits of thinking.

Heavenly Father, thank You for my brain, a gift
from You. Help me focus on things that honor You.
Open my eyes to beautiful, positive things—
and, most important, to Your truth. Amen.

Day 196

SHAKE IT UP!

The LORD had said to Abram, "Leave your native
country, your relatives, and your father's family,
and go to the land that I will show you. . . . I will
bless you. . .and you will be a blessing to others."
GENESIS 12:1–2 NLT

In God's wisdom, He likes to shake us up a little, stretch
us out of our comfort zone, push us out on a limb. Yet
we resist the change, cling to what's known, and try to
change His mind with fat, sloppy tears. Are you facing
a big change? God wants us to be willing to embrace
change He brings into our lives. Even unbidden change.
You may feel as if you're out on a limb, but don't forget
that God is the tree trunk. He's not going to let you fall.

Holy, loving Father, in every area of my life,
teach me to trust You more deeply. Amen.

Day 197

MARVELOUS THUNDER

*"God's voice thunders in marvelous ways; he does
great things beyond our understanding."*

JOB 37:5 NIV

Have you ever reflected deeply on the power that God
is? Not that He *has*, but that He is.

Consider this: The One who controls nature also
holds every one of our tears in His hand. He is our Father,
and He works on our behalf. He is more than enough
to meet our needs; He does things far beyond what our
human minds can understand. This One who is power
loves you. He looks at you and says, *"I delight in you, My
daughter."* Wow! His ways are marvelous and beyond
understanding.

*Lord God, You are power. You hold all things in Your
hand and You chose to love me. You see my actions,
hear my thoughts, watch my heartbreak. . .and You
still love me. Please help me trust in Your
power, never my own. Amen.*

Day 198

MASTERPIECE

You made all the delicate, inner parts of my body
and knit me together in my mother's womb.
PSALM 139:13 NLT

At the moment of your conception, roughly three million decisions were made about you. Everything from your eye color and the number of your wisdom teeth to the shape of your nose and the swirl of your fingerprints was determined in the blink of an eye. God is a big God. Unfathomable. Incomparable. Frankly, words just don't do Him justice. And He made *you*. You were knit together by a one-of-a-kind, amazing God who is absolutely, undeniably, head-over-heels crazy-in-love with you. Try to wrap your brain around that.

Heavenly Father and Creator, thank You for
the amazing gift of life, for my uniqueness
and individuality. Help me use my life
as a gift of praise to You. Amen.

Day 199

POWER UP

*The Spirit of God, who raised Jesus
from the dead, lives in you.*
ROMANS 8:11 NLT

God is the same yesterday, today, and forever. His strength does not diminish over time. That same mountain-moving power you read about in the lives of people from the Old and New Testaments still exists today. We don't have to go it alone. Our heavenly Father wants to help. All we have to do is ask. He has already made His power available to His children. Whatever we face, wherever we go, whatever dreams we have for our lives, take courage and know that anything is possible when we draw on the power of God.

*Father, help me remember that You are always
with me, ready to help me do all things. Amen.*

Day 200

INTO GOD'S PRESENCE

"That person can pray to God and find favor with him, they will see God's face and shout for joy."

JOB 33:26 NIV

Prayer is the channel through which God's grace flows. We do not pray because God needs us to pray; we pray because we need to pray. When we come into God's presence, we are renewed. Our hearts lift. We look into the face of the One who loves us most, and we are filled with joy.

Father, thank You for the gift of prayer and the promise that I can talk with You at any time. As I look to You, fill my heart with Your joy. Amen.

Day 201

REACH OUT TO OTHERS

Whoever has the gift of encouraging
others should encourage.

ROMANS 12:8 NCV

Just as God encourages us, He wants us to encourage others. The word *encourage* comes from Latin words that mean "to put heart or inner strength into someone." When God encourages us, His own heart reaches out to us and His strength becomes ours. As we rely on His grace, we are empowered to turn and reach out to those around us, lending them our hearts and strength.

Lord, thank You for reaching out to me with Your heart
and giving me Your strength. I pray that I would use
that strength to encourage others. Amen.

Day 202

WHEN GOD'S PEOPLE PRAY

Pray for the peace of Jerusalem:
"May those who love you be secure."
PSALM 122:6 NIV

God, in all His power, has invited us to come alongside Him. He's asked us to join Him in His work by praying for each other.

For centuries, God's people have been treated unfairly and unjustly. Yet we've survived when other groups haven't. The reason we've survived when so many have sought to silence us is because we have something our enemies don't have. We have the power of God behind us.

When we pray, we call upon every resource available to us, as the children of God. We call upon His strength, His compassion, His ferocity, His mercy, His love, and His justice. We have the ability to extend God's reach to the other side of our town or the other side of the world, all because we pray.

Dear Father, thank You for letting me join You in
Your work. Please bless the people who love You,
wherever they are in this world. Allow them to
prosper according to their love for You. Amen.

Day 203

HOW ABOUT SOME FUN?

A twinkle in the eye means joy in the heart,
and good news makes you feel fit as a fiddle.
PROVERBS 15:30 MSG

God does not want His kids to be worn out and stressed out. A little relaxation, recreation—and, yes—*fun* are essential components of a balanced life. Even Jesus and His disciples found it necessary to get away from the crowds and pressures of ministry to rest. There's a lot of fun to be had out there—playing tennis or golf, jogging, swimming, painting, knitting, playing a musical instrument, visiting an art gallery, playing a board game, or going to a movie, a play, or a football game. Have you had any fun this week?

Lord, You are the One who gives balance to my life.
Help me to find time today for a little relaxation,
recreation, and even fun. Amen.

Day 204

GOD'S MOUNTAIN SANCTUARY

And seeing the multitudes, he went up into a
mountain. . .and. . .his disciples came unto him:
and he opened his mouth, and taught them.
MATTHEW 5:1–2 KJV

Jesus often retreated to a mountain to pray. There He called His disciples to depart from the multitudes so that He could teach them valuable truths—the lessons we learn from nature. Do you yearn for a place where problems evaporate like the morning dew? Do you need a place of solace? God is wherever you are—behind a bedroom door, nestled alongside you in your favorite chair, or even standing at a sink full of dirty dishes. Come away and enter God's mountain sanctuary.

Heavenly Father, I long to hear Your voice and to
flow in the path You clear before me. Help me find
sanctuary in Your abiding presence. Amen.

Day 205

HANNAH'S PRAYER

"The eyes of the Lord search the whole earth
in order to strengthen those whose hearts
are fully committed to him."

2 CHRONICLES 16:9 NLT

Hannah was barren. She prayed before God with a broken heart and promised God that if He gave her a child, she would commit him to the Lord all the days of his life. God heard and answered her prayer. God granted Hannah a male child whom she named Samuel. She only had Samuel for a short time before she took him to Eli, the priest. Samuel was not an ordinary child. He heard the voice of God at a very young age. He grew up to become a judge and prophet that could not be matched in all of Israel's history.

God is looking for ordinary men and women whose prayers reflect hearts completely committed to Him. He found such commitment in Hannah, and He answered her prayer.

Father, may my prayers reflect a deep commitment
to You and may all that I ask for be for Your
kingdom and not for my own glory. Amen.

Day 206

BREATHING

*In certain ways we are weak, but the Spirit is here
to help us. For example, when we don't know
what to pray for, the Spirit prays for us in
ways that cannot be put into words.*

ROMANS 8:26 CEV

The Holy Spirit is the wind that blows through our world, breathing grace and life into everything that exists. He will breathe through you also as you open yourself to Him. We need not worry about our own weakness or mistakes, for the Spirit will make up for them. His creative power will pray through us, work through us, and love through us.

*Holy Spirit, thank You for interceding on my behalf,
for breathing grace and life into me. Even through
my weakness, thank You for Your power that
carries my very breath to God. Amen.*

Day 207

HE WILL SEND HELP

*"The waves of death swirled about me; the torrents
of destruction overwhelmed me.... In my distress
I called to the LORD.... From his temple he
heard my voice; my cry came to his ears."*

2 SAMUEL 22:5, 7 NIV

God never asked us to do life alone. When the waves
of death swirl around us and the pounding rain of
destruction threatens to overwhelm us, we can cry out
to our heavenly Father, knowing He will not let us drown.
He will hear our voice, and He will send help. So, next
time you feel that you can't put one foot in front of the
other, ask God to send you His strength and energy. He
will help you live out your purpose in this chaotic world.

*Lord, thank You for strengthening me when
the "dailyness" of life and its various trials
threaten to overwhelm me. Amen.*

Day 208

LADIES IN WAITING

I will wait for the LORD. . . . I will put my trust in him.
ISAIAH 8:17 NIV

Do we want joy without accepting heartache? Peace without living through the stress? Patience without facing demands? God sees things differently. He's giving us the opportunity to learn through these delays, irritations, and struggles. Like Isaiah, we need to learn the art of waiting on God. He will come through every time—but in *His* time, not ours. The wait may be hours or days, or it could be years. But God is always faithful to provide for us. It is when we learn to wait on Him that we will find joy, peace, and patience through the struggle.

Father, You know what I need, so I will wait. Help me be patient, knowing You control my situation and that all good things come in Your time. Amen.

Day 209

THE DREAM MAKER

"What no eye has seen, what no ear has heard, and what no human mind has conceived"—the things God has prepared for those who love him.
1 CORINTHIANS 2:9 NIV

Dreams, goals, and expectations are part of our daily lives. We have an idea of what we want and how we're going to achieve it. Disappointment can raise its ugly head when what we wanted—what we expected—doesn't happen like we thought it should or doesn't happen as fast as we planned. God knows the dreams He has placed inside of you. He created you and knows what you can do—even better than you know yourself. Maintain your focus—not on the dream but on the Dream Maker—and together you will achieve your dream.

God, thank You for putting dreams in my heart. I refuse to quit. I'm looking to You to show me how to reach my dreams. Amen.

Day 210

LAUGH OUT LOUD

*"He will once again fill your mouth with laughter
and your lips with shouts of joy."*

JOB 8:21 NLT

Did you know God wants to make you laugh? He wants to
fill you with loud, rowdy joy. Oh, some days His grace will
come to you quietly and calmly. But every now and then
you will have days when He makes you laugh out loud.

*Heavenly Father, the gift of laughter is such
a blessing. Help me to look for reasons to
laugh out loud with Your joy. Amen.*

Day 211

THE NEXT OASIS

The LORD will always guide you and provide good things to eat when you are in the desert. He will make you healthy. You will be like a garden that has plenty of water or like a stream that never runs dry.

ISAIAH 58:11 CEV

God wants you to be healthy—not just physically, but emotionally, intellectually, and spiritually as well. He wants to fill your life full of all the things you truly need. The life He wants for you is not dry and empty and barren. Instead, it is lush and full of delicious things to nourish you. We all have to cross life's deserts sometimes, but even then God will supply what you need to reach the next oasis He has waiting.

Lord, this life can feel like an incredibly long journey, especially when I am in the desert. Sustain and strengthen me with the promises of Your Word. Amen.

Day 212

LIFE'S CIRCUMSTANCES

My child, do not reject the LORD's discipline,
and don't get angry when he corrects you.
The LORD corrects those he loves, just as
parents correct the child they delight in.

PROVERBS 3:11–12 NCV

God doesn't send us to time-out, and He certainly doesn't
take us over His knee and spank us. Instead, His discipline
comes to us through the circumstances of life. By saying
yes to whatever we face, no matter how difficult and
frustrating it may be, we allow God's grace to infuse
each moment of our day. We may be surprised to find
that even in life's most discouraging moments, God's
love was waiting all along.

Father, it can be difficult to accept Your discipline.
Help me to recognize when You are correcting
me and to see it as an outpouring of Your
love and Your delight. Amen.

Day 213

COMFORT FOOD

*For whatever things were written before were written
for our learning, that we through the patience and
comfort of the Scriptures might have hope.*

ROMANS 15:4 NKJV

Romans 15:4 tells us that the scriptures are comfort food
for the soul. They were written and given so that, through
our learning, we would be comforted with the truths of
God. Worldly pleasures bring a temporary comfort, but
the problem still remains when the pleasure or comfort
fades. The words of God are soothing, however, and
provide permanent hope and peace. Through God's
Word you will be changed, and your troubles will dim in
the bright light of Christ. So the next time you are sad,
lonely, or disappointed, turn to the Word of God as your
source of comfort.

*Thank You, Father, for the rich comfort Your Word
provides. Help me remember to find my comfort
in scripture rather than through earthly things
that will ultimately fail me. Amen.*

Day 214

GOOD FOR YOU!

A happy heart is like good medicine,
but a broken spirit drains your strength.

PROVERBS 17:22 NCV

God longs to make you happy. He knows that happiness is good for you. Mentally and physically, you function better when you are happy. Discouragement and sadness sap your strength. It's like trying to work while carrying a heavy load on your back: it slows you down and makes everything harder. Let God heal the breaks in your spirit. His grace can make you strong and happy.

Father, I know the heaviness of a broken spirit.
Heal me and help me carry my burdens.
Remind me of the reasons I have to
be grateful and happy. Amen.

Day 215

JUMPING HURDLES

God's way is perfect. All the LORD's promises prove true.
PSALM 18:30 NLT

Maybe there are times when you just don't think you can take one more disappointment or hurt. That's the perfect time to draw strength from God and His Word. Meditate on encouraging scriptures, or play a song that you know strengthens your heart and mind. Ask God to infuse you with His strength, and you'll find the power to take another step, and another—until you find yourself on the other side of that challenge you're facing today.

God, give me strength each day to face the obstacles
I am to overcome. I am thankful I don't
have to face them alone. Amen.

Day 216

CHRISTLIKE

Don't sin by letting anger control you.
Think about it overnight and remain silent.
PSALM 4:4 NLT

A disciple must practice certain skills until she becomes good at them. As Christ's disciples, we are called to live like Him. The challenge of that calling is often hardest in life's small, daily frustrations, especially with the people we love the most. But as we practice saying no to anger, controlling it rather than allowing it to control us, God's grace helps us develop new skills, even ones we never thought possible!

God, teach me the difference between sinful anger and
righteous anger. Help me to push the PAUSE button
when I get angry so I can listen to You. Amen.

Day 217

PEOPLE PLEASER VS. GOD PLEASER

*We are not trying to please people
but God, who tests our hearts.*

1 THESSALONIANS 2:4 NIV

When we allow ourselves to be real before God, it doesn't matter what others think. If the God of the universe has accepted us, then who cares about someone else's opinion? It is impossible to please both God and man. We must make a choice. Man looks at the outward appearance, but God looks at the heart. Align your heart with His. Let go of impression management that focuses on outward appearance. Receive God's unconditional love and enjoy the freedom to be yourself before Him!

*Dear Lord, may I live for You alone. Help me transition
from a people pleaser to a God pleaser. Amen.*

Day 218

A HEAVENLY PARTY

"I tell you that in the same way there will be more rejoicing in heaven over one sinner who repents than over ninety-nine righteous persons who do not need to repent."

LUKE 15:7 NIV

The Father threw your very own party the moment you accepted His Son as your Savior. Did you experience a taste of that party from the response of your spiritual mentors here on earth? As Christians, we should celebrate with our new brothers and sisters in Christ every chance we get. If you haven't yet taken that step in your faith, don't wait! Heaven's party planners are eager to get your celebration started.

Father, I am so grateful that You rejoice in new Christians. Strengthen my desire to reach the lost while I am here on earth. Then, when I reach heaven, the heavenly parties will be all the sweeter! Amen.

Day 219

WHEN I THINK OF THE HEAVENS

When I consider your heavens, the work of your fingers,
the moon and the stars, which you have set in place,
what is mankind that you are mindful of them,
human beings that you care for them?
PSALM 8:3-4 NIV

Daughter of God, you are important to your heavenly Father, more important than the sun, the moon, and the stars. You are created in the image of God, and He cares for you. In fact, He cares so much that He sent His Son, Jesus, to offer His life as a sacrifice for your sins. The next time you look up at the heavens, the next time you ooh and aah over a majestic mountain or emerald waves crashing against the shoreline, remember that those things, in all their splendor, don't even come close to you—God's greatest creation.

O Father, when I look at everything You have created,
I'm so overwhelmed with who You are. Who am I that
You would think twice about me? And yet You do.
You love me, and for that I'm eternally grateful! Amen.

Day 220

SING!

*But each day the L*ORD *pours his unfailing love
upon me, and through each night I sing his
songs, praying to God who gives me life.*

PSALM 42:8 NLT

Life itself is a gift of grace. The very blood that flows through our veins, the beat of our hearts, and the steady hum of our metabolism—all of that is God's free gift to us, a token of His constant and unconditional love. When we are so richly loved, how can we help but sing, even in the darkness?

*Dear Lord, Giver of blessing, Giver of life, as I
experience Your unfailing love each and every day,
teach my heart to sing Your joyful song. Amen.*

Day 221

DIFFICULT PEOPLE

Do not turn your freedom into an opportunity for
the flesh, but through love serve one another.
GALATIANS 5:13 NASB

Sometimes, like David, we need to turn our skirmishes with others over to the Lord. Then, by using our weapons—God's Word and a steadfast faith—we need to love and forgive others as God loves and forgives us. Although we may not like to admit it, we have all said and done some pretty awful things ourselves, making the lives of others difficult. Yet God has forgiven us *and* continues to love us. So do the right thing. Pull your feet out of the mire of unforgiveness, sidestep verbal retaliation, and stand tall in the freedom of love and forgiveness.

The words and deeds of others have left me wounded
and bleeding. Forgiveness and love seem to be the
last thing on my mind. Change my heart, Lord.
Help me to love and forgive others as
You love and forgive me. Amen.

Day 222

UNCHAINED!

The Spirit you received does not make you slaves,
so that you live in fear again; rather, the Spirit you
received brought about your adoption to sonship.
And by him we cry, "Abba, Father."
ROMANS 8:15 NIV

Do you struggle with fear? Do you feel it binding you
with its invisible chains? If so, then there's good news.
Through Jesus, you have received the Spirit of sonship. A
son (or daughter) of the most-high God has nothing to fear.
Knowing you've been set free is enough to make you cry,
"Abba, Father!" in praise. Today, acknowledge your fears
to the Lord. He will loose your chains and set you free.

Lord, thank You that You are the great chain breaker!
I don't have to live in fear. I am Your child, Your
daughter, and You are my Daddy-God! Amen.

Day 223

JUST IN TIME

Therefore let us [with privilege] approach the throne of grace [that is, the throne of God's gracious favor] with confidence and without fear, so that we may receive mercy [for our failures] and find [His amazing] grace to help in time of need [an appropriate blessing, coming just at the right moment].
HEBREWS 4:16 AMP

As believers, our lives become exciting when we wait on God to direct our paths, because He knows what is best for us at any given moment. His plans and agenda are never wrong.

Once we fully realize He knows best and turn our lives over to the Spirit for direction, we can allow God to be in charge of our calendar; His timing is what is paramount.

When chomping at the bit for a job offer or for a proposal, His timing might seem slow. "Hurry up, God!" we groan. But when we learn to wait patiently on His promises, we will see the plans He has for us are more than we dared hope—or dream. God promises to answer us; and it never fails to be just in time.

Lord, I want Your perfect will in my life.
Help me learn to wait upon You. Amen.

Day 224

SENDING GOD'S FAVOR

You help us by your prayers. Then many will give thanks on our behalf for the gracious favor granted us in answer to the prayers of many.

2 CORINTHIANS 1:11 NIV

The power of prayer is better in a crisis than a casserole. It's better than being there, holding someone's hand or doing their laundry. The power of prayer does more for a missionary on the other side of the world than a box of clothes or even a check.

Prayer brings peace. Prayer brings wisdom and clarity. Prayer is powerful.

Next time we offer to pray for someone, we can say it with the confidence that our prayers will be heard. They will be answered. And they will make a beautiful difference in the lives of those for whom we pray.

Dear Father, thank You for hearing my prayers. Thank You for showing favor to others at my request. Amen.

Day 225

WEB OF LOVE

*"So now I am giving you a new commandment:
Love each other. Just as I have loved you,
you should love each other."*

JOHN 13:34 NLT

God's grace comes to us through a net of relationships and connections. Because we know we are totally and unconditionally loved, we can in turn love others. The connections between us grow ever wider and stronger, a web of love that unites us all with God.

Jesus, I am grateful for the relationships You have given me. Thank You for Your love that enables me to love and be loved by others. Amen.

Day 226

KING FOREVER

You, O God, are my king from ages past,
bringing salvation to the earth.
PSALM 74:12 NLT

Sometimes it seems like every part of our lives is affected by change. Nothing ever seems to stay the same. These changes can leave us feeling unsteady in the present and uncertain about the future. It's different in God's kingdom. He's the King now, just as He was in the days of Abraham. His reign will continue until the day His Son returns to earth, and then on into eternity. We can rely—absolutely depend on—His unchanging nature. Take comfort in the stability of the King—He's our leader now and forever!

Almighty King, You are my Rock. When my world
is in turmoil and changes swirl around me,
You are my anchor and my center of balance.
Thank You for never changing. Amen.

Day 227

GO OUT WITH JOY

For ye shall go out with joy, and be led forth with
peace: the mountains and the hills shall break
forth before you into singing, and all the
trees of the field shall clap their hands.

ISAIAH 55:12 KJV

God reveals Himself in a million different ways, but perhaps the most breathtaking is through nature. The next time you're in a mountainous spot, pause and listen. Can you hear the sound of God's eternal song? Does joy radiate through your being? Aren't you filled with wonder and with peace? The Lord has, through the beauty of nature, given us a rare and glorious gift.

When I view the wonders of Your marvelous creation,
Lord, my heart fills with absolute joy! Amen.

Day 228

YOUR HEAVENLY FATHER

The LORD's love never ends; his mercies never stop.
They are new every morning; LORD, your loyalty is great.
LAMENTATIONS 3:22-23 NCV

Regardless of your relationship with your earthly father, your heavenly Father loves you with an *unfailing love*. He is faithful to walk with you through the ups and downs of life. Remember that every day is a day to honor your heavenly Father. Begin and end today praising Him for who He is. Express thanksgiving. Present your requests to Him. Tell Him how much you love Him. God longs to be your Abba Father, a loving Daddy to you, His daughter!

Father, thank You for being a loving God,
my Abba Father, my Redeemer. Amen.

Day 229

FIX YOUR THOUGHTS ON TRUTH

And now, dear brothers and sisters, one final thing.
Fix your thoughts on what is true, and honorable,
and right, and pure, and lovely, and admirable.
Think about things that are excellent
and worthy of praise.
PHILIPPIANS 4:8 NLT

Dig through the scriptures and find truths from God's Word to combat any false message that you may be struggling with. Write them down and memorize them. Here are a few to get started:

God looks at my heart, not my outward appearance. (1 Samuel 16:7)

I am free in Christ. (1 Corinthians 1:30)

I am a new creation in Christ. My old self is gone! (2 Corinthians 5:17)

The next time you feel negativity and false messages slip into your thinking, fix your thoughts on what you know to be true. Pray for the Lord to replace the doubts and negativity with His words of truth.

Lord God, please control my thoughts and help
me set my mind and heart on You alone. Amen.

Day 230

THE TREES THAT CATCH
THE STORM

*Brothers and sisters, I could not address you as people
who live by the Spirit but as people who are still
worldly—mere infants in Christ. I gave you milk,
not solid food, for you were not yet ready for
it. Indeed, you are still not ready.*

1 CORINTHIANS 3:1-2 NIV

Think of the healthiest trees that shoot up from the forest
floor. . .they stretch toward the sun and spread their
branches wide. But when the storms of life blow through,
many times it's those towering oaks that will catch the
brunt of the wind. The last thing the enemy of your soul
wants is for you to grow in Christ and His wisdom. So
expect storms, and be watchful and ready. But remember
that we can stand strong like the oak trees. We can know
peace in the midst of the gale. For Christ is the strength
in our branches and the light that gives us life!

*Jesus, help me to grow strong in the rich,
nourishing soil of Your love and grace.
Make me a warrior for Your cause. Amen.*

Day 231

A STRONG HEART

*Whom have I in heaven but you? And earth has nothing
I desire besides you. My flesh and my heart may
fail, but God is the strength of my heart
and my portion forever.*

PSALM 73:25–26 NIV

You don't have to be strong. In your weakness, God's
strength shines through. And His strength surpasses
anything you could produce, even on your best day.
It's the same strength that spoke the heavens and the
earth into existence. The same strength that parted
the Red Sea. And it's the same strength that made the
journey up the hill to the cross. So how do you tap into
that strength? There's really only one way. Come into
His presence. Spend some quiet time with Him. Allow
His strong arms to encompass you. God is all you will
ever need.

*Father, I feel so weak at times. It's hard just to put
one foot in front of the other. But I know You
are my strength. Invigorate me with
that strength today, Lord. Amen.*

Day 232

PUT ON LOVE

And over all these virtues put on love,
which binds them all together in perfect unity.
COLOSSIANS 3:14 NIV

There is one accessory that always fits, always looks right, always is appropriate, and always makes us more attractive to others. When we wear it, we are beautiful. When we wear it, we become more popular, more sought-after, more admired. What is that accessory, you ask, and where can you buy it? It's love, and you can't buy it anywhere. But it's free, and it's always available through the Holy Spirit. When we call on Him to help us love others, He cloaks us in a beautiful covering that draws people to us and makes us perfectly lovely in every way.

Dear Father, as I get dressed each day,
help me to remember the most important
accessory I can wear is Your love. Amen.

Day 233

LOVING THE UNLOVABLE

"You have heard the law that says, 'Love your neighbor' and hate your enemy. But I say, love your enemies! Pray for those who persecute you! In that way, you will be acting as true children of your Father in heaven."

MATTHEW 5:43–45 NLT

Sometimes running into a difficult person can actually be a "divine appointment"! Maybe you're the only person they'll see all week who wears a smile on her face. When you happen upon a difficult person whom you'd rather not talk to, take the time to pray for your attitude and then pray for that person. Greet them with a smile and look them in the eye. There is no reason to fear difficult people if you trust in God. He will show you what to do and say as you listen to His promptings (Luke 12:12).

Heavenly Father, I pray that You would help me not to shy away from the people You have allowed to cross my path. Help me speak Your truth and share Your love boldly. Amen.

Day 234

ENCOURAGE OTHERS

Worry weighs a person down;
an encouraging word cheers a person up.
PROVERBS 12:25 NLT

There is so much sorrow in this world. At any given time, there are many people within your sphere of influence who are hurting. Worry weighs them down as they face disappointment, loss, and other trials. Think about how much it means to you when someone takes the time to encourage you. Do the same for others. Be the voice of encouragement. There is blessing to be found in lifting up those around you.

Father, as I go through this week, make me
an encourager. Provide opportunities for me to
encourage those around me. I truly desire to cheer
up the hearts of those who are worried. Amen.

Day 235

PRAYING TOGETHER

For where two or three are gathered together in
my name, there am I in the midst of them.
MATTHEW 18:20 KJV

Of all the passages in the Bible that emphasize the importance of gathering for worship and prayer, this one stands out. It is short and sweet and to the point. Why should we gather together to pray with other Christians? Because when we do, *God shows up!* The Lord is in our midst.

As you gather with other Christians in your church or even in your family, God is honored. He loves to listen to the hearts and voices of His children unified in prayer. He will be faithful to answer according to His perfect will.

Father, thank You for the promise that where we
gather in Your name, there You will be also.
Help me never to give up the practice of
praying with fellow believers. Amen.

Day 236

RECIPROCAL

When we get together, I want to encourage you in your faith, but I also want to be encouraged by yours.

ROMANS 1:12 NLT

Encouragement is always reciprocal. When we encourage others, we are ourselves encouraged. In the world's economy, we pay a price in order to receive something we want; in other words, we give up something to get something. But in God's economy we always get back what we give up. We are connected to each other, like parts of a body. Whatever good things we do for another are good for us as well.

God, thank You for the encouragement I find from my brothers and sisters in You. Help me to both share and receive the encouragement of Your love. Amen.

Day 237

BE HAPPY!

Blessed are those who act justly,
who always do what is right.
PSALM 106:3 NIV

In the world we live in today, some might think a bank error or a mistake on a bill in their favor would be justification for keeping the money without a word. But a true Christ follower would not look at these kinds of situations as good or fortunate events. Our happiness is being honest, doing what is right, because that happiness is the promised spiritual reward. Because we want to be blessed by God, to be a happy follower of Him, we will always seek to do what is right.

Gracious and heavenly Father, thank You for Your
blessings each and every day. I am thankful to be
Your follower. When I am tempted to do something
that would displease You, remind me that You
will bless me if I act justly. My happiness will be
a much better reward. In Your name, amen.

Day 238

STANDING IN THE LIGHT

Though I have fallen, I will rise. Though I sit in darkness, the LORD will be my light.

MICAH 7:8 NIV

We may fall down, but God will lift us up. We may feel surrounded by darkness on every side, but He will be our light, guiding the way, showing us which step to take next. No matter where we are, what we've done, or what we're facing, God is our Rescuer, our Savior, and our Friend.

Satan wants to convince us that we have no hope, no future. But God's children always have a future and a hope. . .we are cherished, and we belong to Him.

Dear Father, thank You for giving me confidence in a future filled with good things. When I'm down, remind me to trust in Your love. Thank You for lifting me out of darkness to stand in Your light. Amen.

Day 239

WHISPERS IN THE WIND

Then Jesus told him, "Because you have seen me,
you have believed; blessed are those who
have not seen and yet have believed."

JOHN 20:29 NIV

We can't see God. We can't take Him by the hand or even converse with Him face-to-face like we do a friend. But we still know He is present in our lives because we can experience the effects. God moves among His people, and we can see it. God speaks to His people, and we can hear the still, small voice. And, just as we can feel the wind across our cheeks, we can feel God's presence. We don't need to see God physically to know He exists and is working.

You are like the wind, Lord. Powerful and fast moving,
soft and gentle. We may not see You, but we can sense
You. Help us believe, even when we can't see. Amen.

Day 240

FILL 'ER UP

"What strength do I have, that I should still hope?"
JOB 6:11 NIV

Run, rush, hurry, dash: a typical American woman's day. It's easy to identify with David's lament in Psalm 22:14 (NASB): "I am poured out like water. . .my heart is like wax; it is melted within me." Translation: I'm pooped; I'm numb; I'm drained dry. When we are at the end of our strength, God doesn't want us to lose hope of the refilling He can provide if we only lift our empty cups to Him.

Fill me up, Lord! I need Your heavenly presence. . .
Your strength. . .Your comfort. Thank You for
the hope You provide in the daily-ness of life!

Day 241

PEACE

*"I will teach all your children,
and they will enjoy great peace."*
ISAIAH 54:13 NLT

It's hard not to worry about the children in our lives. Many dangers threaten them, and our world is so uncertain. We can do our best to teach and guide the children we love, but in the end we must trust them to God's grace, knowing they must find their own relationship with Him—and as they know Him, they will find peace, even in the midst of the world's uncertainty.

Heavenly Father, thank You for the children in my life. Help me remember that You love them even more than I do and that You hold them in Your loving arms. Amen.

Day 242

KEEP BREATHING, SISTER!

As long as we are alive, we still have hope,
just as a live dog is better off than a dead lion.
ECCLESIASTES 9:4 CEV

Isn't this a tremendous scripture? At first glance, the ending elicits a chuckle. But consider the truth it contains: Regardless of how powerful, regal, or intimidating a lion is, when he's dead, he's dead. But the living—you and I—still have hope. Limitless possibilities! Hope for today and for the future. Although we may be as lowly dogs, fresh, juicy bones abound. As long as we're breathing, it's not too late!

God of possibilities, remind me it's never too late as
long as I'm breathing. Because of You, I have hope!

Day 243

A GOOD MORSEL

Taste and see that the LORD is good;
blessed is the one who takes refuge in him.
PSALM 34:8 NIV

The world gives the idea to nonbelievers that God isn't worth a taste. The world emphasizes a self-focus, while the Lord says put others before self and God before all. In reality, to walk and talk with God is the best thing you can do for yourself. As you walk with God, learning to pray and lean on Him and operate in His will, you are storing up treasures for yourself in heaven. In the world, you are demonstrating the love of Christ and being an influence to get others to taste of the Lord.

Like so many foods that are good for us, all it requires is that first taste, a tiny morsel, which whets the appetite for more of Him. Then you can be open to all the goodness, all the fullness of the Lord.

Lord, fill my cup to overflowing with Your love
so that it pours out of me in a way that makes
others want what I have. Amen.

Day 244

SAFE IN CHRIST

This is what God commands: that we believe in his
Son, Jesus Christ, and that we love each
other, just as he commanded.

1 JOHN 3:23 NCV

Again and again, the Bible links faith and love. Our
human tendency is to put up walls of selfishness around
ourselves, to protect ourselves at all costs. God asks us
instead to believe daily that we are safe in Christ and to
allow ourselves to be vulnerable as we reach out in love
to those around us.

Father God, Your commands are not burdensome.
You ask me to believe in Your Son and to love others.
Give me the grace to obey You with all my heart. Amen.

Day 245

THE LORD HIMSELF
GOES BEFORE YOU

*"The Lord himself goes before you and will be with
you; he will never leave you nor forsake you.
Do not be afraid; do not be discouraged."*

DEUTERONOMY 31:8 NIV

Joshua 1:9 (NIV) tells us to "be strong and courageous. Do
not be afraid; do not be discouraged, for the Lord your
God will be with you wherever you go." Be encouraged!
Even when it feels like it, you are truly never alone. And
never without access to God's power. If you've trusted
Christ as your Savior, the Spirit of God Himself is alive
and well and working inside you at all times. What an
astounding miracle! The Creator of the universe dwells
within you and is available to encourage you and help
you make right choices on a moment-by-moment basis.

*Thank You, Lord, for the incredible gift of Your
presence in each and every situation I face.
Allow me to remember this and to call upon
Your name as I go about each day.*

Day 246

CARTWHEELS OF JOY

*I'm singing joyful praise to God. I'm turning cartwheels
of joy to my Savior God. Counting on God's Rule to
prevail, I take heart and gain strength. I run like
a deer. I feel like I'm king of the mountain!*
HABAKKUK 3:18–19 MSG

What would happen if we followed the advice of the
psalmist and turned a cartwheel of joy in our hearts—
regardless of the circumstances—then leaned into and
trusted His rule to prevail? Think of the happiness and
peace that could be ours with a total surrender to God's
care. Taking a giant step, armed with scriptures and
praise and joy, we can surmount any obstacle put before
us, running like a deer, climbing the tall mountains. With
God at our side, it's possible to be king of the mountain.

*Dear Lord, I need Your help. Gently guide me
so I might learn to lean on You and become
confident in Your care. Amen.*

Day 247

THE ULTIMATE ACT OF LOVE

*Bring joy to your servant, Lord, for I put my trust
in you. You, Lord, are forgiving and good,
abounding in love to all who call to you.*

PSALM 86:4–5 NIV

Forgiveness doesn't require that the person who did the
hurting apologize or acknowledge what they've done. It's
not about making the score even. It doesn't even require
forgetting about the incident. But it is about admitting
that the one who hurt us is human, just as we are. We
surrender our right for revenge and, like God, let go and
give the wrongdoer mercy, therefore blessing them.

*Gracious and loving Father, thank You that You love
me and have forgiven me of my sins. May I be more
like You in forgiving others. Although I may not be able
to forgive as easily as You do, please encourage me to
take those small steps. In forgiving others, Father,
I am that much closer to being like You. Amen.*

Day 248

PRAYING THE MIND OF CHRIST

We demolish arguments and every pretension that sets itself up against the knowledge of God, and we take captive every thought to make it obedient to Christ.

2 CORINTHIANS 10:5 NIV

By reading and praying scripture and using positive statements in our prayers that claim what God has already said He will do for us, the mind of Christ is being activated in us. By taking captive every thought, we learn to know what thought is of God, what belongs to us, and what is of the enemy. Recognize, take captive, and bind up the thoughts that are of the enemy and throw them out! The more we commune with God, fellowship with Him, and learn from Him, the more we cultivate the mind of Christ.

Lord, help me identify the thoughts that are not Your thoughts and purge them. I know that soon Your thoughts will be the ones I hear, and not the enemy's. In this way I will hear You more clearly so I may be an obedient disciple. Amen!

Day 249

I GROW WEARY

But those who wait for the LORD [who expect, look for, and hope in Him] will gain new strength and renew their power; they will lift up their wings [and rise up close to God] like eagles [rising toward the sun]; they will run and not become weary, they will walk and not grow tired.

ISAIAH 40:31 AMP

As long as we are warring inside, we will not find rest. We must find out what Jesus wants for our lives and then obey. Feasting on His Word and learning more about Him will give us the direction we need and the ability to trust. It is only when we understand our salvation and surrender that we can come to Him, unencumbered by guilt or fear, and lay our head on His chest. Safe within His embrace, we can rest. We will be as a well-watered garden, refreshed and blessed by our loving Creator.

Father, I am weary and need Your refreshing Spirit to guide me. I trust in You. Amen.

Day 250

GRACE MULTIPLIED

Honor the LORD with your wealth and with
the best part of everything you produce.
PROVERBS 3:9 NLT

We connect the word *wealth* with money, but long ago the word meant "happiness, prosperity, well-being." If you think about your wealth in this light, then the word encompasses far more of your life. Your health, your abilities, your friends, your family, your physical strength, and your creative energy—all of these are parts of your true wealth. Grace brought all of these riches into your life, and when we use them to honor God, grace is multiplied still more.

Father, when I consider all the good things You have given me, I am rich beyond belief. Help me to graciously honor You with my wealth. Amen.

Day 251

LETTING GO

A peaceful heart leads to a healthy body;
jealousy is like cancer in the bones.
PROVERBS 14:30 NLT

Some emotions are meant to be nourished, and others
need to be quickly dropped into God's hands. Learn to
cultivate and seek out that which brings peace to your
heart. And practice letting go of your negative feelings
as quickly as you can, releasing them to God. If you cling
to these dark feelings, they will reproduce like a cancer,
blocking the healthy flow of grace into your life.

O God, search me and know my heart. Expose any
negative feelings in me. Help me leave them
at the cross. Cleanse me and fill my
heart with Your peace. Amen.

Day 252

GOD'S GOOD AND PERFECT WILL

*We continually ask God to fill you
with the knowledge of his will through all the
wisdom and understanding that the Spirit gives.*

COLOSSIANS 1:9 NIV

The apostle Paul reminded the Colossians that he was continuously praying for them to be filled with the knowledge of God's will. Christians have received the Holy Spirit as their Counselor and Guide. Those who do not have a personal relationship with Christ are lacking the Spirit, and thus, they are not able to discern God's will for their lives. Always take advantage of the wonderful gift you have been given. If you have accepted Christ as your Savior, you also have the Spirit. One of the greatest things about the Holy Spirit is that He helps us to distinguish God's call on our life from the other voices of the world. Pray that God will reveal His good and perfect will for your life.

*God, help me draw upon the wonderful resources
I have as a Christian. Help me, through the power
of the Holy Spirit, to know Your will. Amen.*

Day 253

REFRESHMENT IN DRY TIMES

"The grass withers and the flowers fall,
but the word of our God endures forever."
ISAIAH 40:8 NIV

Sometimes our lives feel just like the grass—dry and listless. Maybe we're in a season where things seem to stand still, and we've tried everything to change our circumstances for the better to no avail. It is during those times that we need to remember the faithfulness of God and the permanence of His Word. His promises to us are many and true! God will never leave us or forsake us; and He will provide for, love, and protect us. And, just like the drought, eventually our personal dry times will give way to a time of growth, refreshment, and beauty.

Dear Lord, help me to remember Your love during
difficult times of dryness. Even though it's sometimes
hard to hear Your voice or be patient during hard
times, please remind me of Your many promises
and remind me to stand firmly on them. You
are everything I need and the refreshment I
seek. Praises to my Living Water! Amen.

Day 254

REAP IN JOY!

Remember this: Whoever sows sparingly will also reap sparingly, and whoever sows generously will also reap generously.

2 Corinthians 9:6 niv

Each of us wants to feel appreciated, and we like to deal with a friendly person. Have you ever worked with a person who seemed to have a perpetually bad attitude? You probably didn't feel particularly encouraged after an encounter with this coworker. Yes, sometimes things go wrong, but your attitude in the thick of it is determined by your expectations. If you expect things to turn out well, you'll generally have a positive mental attitude. Treat everyone with genuine kindness, courtesy, and respect, and that is what will be reflected back to you.

Heavenly Father, help me plant the seeds of patience, love, compassion, and courtesy in all those I come in contact with. Please let me make an eternal difference in these people's lives. I want to joyfully reap a rich harvest for Your kingdom. Amen!

Day 255

HEAVEN'S PERSPECTIVE

*Always give yourselves fully to the work of
the Lord, because you know that your labor
in the Lord is not in vain.*

1 Corinthians 15:58 niv

You may feel sometimes as though all of your hard work
comes to nothing. But if your work is the Lord's work,
you can trust Him to bring it to fulfillment. You may not
always know what is being accomplished in the light of
eternity, but God knows. And when you look back from
heaven's perspective, you will be able to see how much
grace was accomplished through all of your hard work.

*God, when I don't see results, I sometimes get
discouraged in my work for You. Help me to remember
that You are busy doing things I cannot see. Amen.*

Day 256

A CONTINUAL FEAST

The cheerful heart has a continual feast.
PROVERBS 15:15 NIV

Our choice of companions has much to do with our outlook. Negativity and positivity are both contagious. The writer of Proverbs says that a cheerful heart has a continual feast. So it's safe to assume that a grumpy heart will feel hungry and lacking, instead of full. While God calls us to minister to those who are hurting, we can do so with discernment. Next time someone complains, ask them to pray with you about their concerns. Tell them a story of how you overcame negativity or repaired a relationship. You might help turn their day around!

God, help me be a positive influence on my friends and family. Give me wisdom and the unwavering hope that comes from Christ, that I may share Your joy with others. Amen.

Day 257

WHY PRAISE GOD?

Though he slay me, yet will I trust in him.
JOB 13:15 KJV

It's difficult to praise God when problems press in harder than a crowd exiting a burning building. But that's the time to praise Him the most. We wait for our circumstances to change, while God desires to change us despite them. Praise coupled with prayer in our darkest moments is what moves the mighty hand of God to work in our hearts and lives. How can we pray and praise God when everything goes wrong? The bigger question might be, How can we not?

*Jesus, help me to pray and praise
You despite my circumstances. Amen.*

Day 258

LOOK UP!

*Your love, LORD, reaches to the heavens,
your faithfulness to the skies.*
PSALM 36:5 NIV

In Bible times people often studied the sky. Looking up at the heavens reminded them of God and His mighty wonders. A rainbow was God's sign to Noah that a flood would never again destroy the earth. God used a myriad of stars to foretell Abraham's abundant family, and a single star heralded Christ's birth. This immense space we call "sky" is a reflection of God's infinite love and faithfulness. So take time today. Look up at the heavens and thank God for His endless love.

*Heavenly Father, remind me to stop and appreciate
Your wonderful creations. And as I look upward,
fill me with Your infinite love. Amen.*

Day 259

THOU SHALT NOT WORRY!

"Do not worry about tomorrow, for tomorrow will worry about itself. Each day has enough trouble of its own."
MATTHEW 6:34 NIV

What if the Lord had written an eleventh commandment: "Thou shalt not worry." In a sense, He did! He commands us in various scriptures not to fret. So cast your anxieties on the Lord. Give them up! Let them go! Don't let worries sap your strength and your joy. Today is a gift from the Lord. Don't sacrifice it to fears and frustrations! Let them go. . .and watch God work!

Father God, lift all anxiety from my heart and make my spirit light again. I know I can't do it on my own. But with You I can let go. . .and watch You work! I praise You, God! Amen.

Day 260

A SOLID FOUNDATION

A bad motive can't achieve a good end.
PROVERBS 17:20 MSG

We hear it all the time: The end justifies the means. But that is not how it works in the kingdom of God. It's like trying to build a beautiful house on a shaky foundation. It just doesn't work. Sooner or later, the weak foundation will affect the rest of the house. True achievement is built on God's grace and love. That is the kind of foundation that holds solid no matter what.

Father, fill my heart with the longing and motivation to do Your work. Help me to build that work on the solid foundation of Your grace and love. Amen.

Day 261

NEVER FAILING...

"My friends scorn me, but I pour out my tears to God."
JOB 16:20 NLT

Sometimes even the best of friends can let you down. Human beings aren't perfect. But God's grace will never fail you. When even your closest friends don't understand you, take your hurt to Him.

Lord, when I feel alone and rejected,
I am so grateful I can pour out my tears to You.
Thank You for Your grace that never fails me. Amen.

Day 262

UNFAILING LOVE

I will instruct you and teach you in the way you should go; I will counsel you with my loving eye on you. . . . Many are the woes of the wicked, but the LORD's unfailing love surrounds the one who trusts in him.

PSALM 32:8, 10 NIV

God's love surrounds us always—if we trust in Him. Have you put your complete trust in the Lord? If not, open your heart to Him and ask Him to become the Lord of your life. Jesus is standing at the door of your heart, ready to come in when you respond (Revelation 3:20). Or maybe you've already accepted Christ as your Savior, but you're not really sure if He can be trusted. Know that He has been faithful to His children through all generations and that He is working out every circumstance in your life for your own good (Romans 8:28).

*Father God, I praise You for Your unfailing love.
Continue to counsel me and lead me in the way
I should go. Thank You for watching over me.
Help me trust You completely. Amen.*

Day 263

AN OFFERING OF JOY

Then my head will be exalted above the enemies who surround me; at his sacred tent I will sacrifice with shouts of joy; I will sing and make music to the Lord.
PSALM 27:6 NIV

It's one thing to offer a sacrifice of joy when things are going your way and people are treating you fairly. But when you've been through a terrible betrayal it's often hard to recapture that feeling of joy. As you face hurts and betrayals, remember that God is the lifter of your head. Sing praises and continue to offer a sacrifice of joy!

Lord, lift my head. Wrap me in Your warm embrace. Help me remember that even though I've experienced betrayal I can still praise You and offer a sacrifice of joy. I love You, Father! Amen.

Day 264

THE END OF YOUR ROPE

*Do not be far from me, for trouble is
near and there is no one to help.*

PSALM 22:11 NIV

Jesus reaches down and wraps you in His loving arms
when you call to Him for help. The Bible tells us He is
close to the brokenhearted (Psalm 34:18). We may not
have the answers we are looking for here in this life, but
we can be sure of this: God sees your pain and loves you
desperately. Call to Him in times of trouble. If you feel
that you're at the end of your rope, look up! His mighty
hand is reaching toward you.

*Heavenly Father, I feel alone and afraid. Surround me
with Your love and give me peace and joy. Amen.*

Day 265

THE DETAILS

She is clothed with strength and dignity,
and she laughs without fear of the future.
PROVERBS 31:25 NLT

God wants to clothe us with His strength, His dignity. He wants us to be whole and competent, full of His grace. When we are, we can look at the future and laugh, knowing God will take care of the details as we trust Him to be the foundation of our lives.

Father, thank You for clothing me with strength
and dignity. Thank You that I can look to my future
without fear, confident You have all the
details in Your hands. Amen.

Day 266

BREATH OF LIFE

He heals the brokenhearted and binds up their wounds
[healing their pain and comforting their sorrow].
Psalm 147:3 AMP

When your life brings disappointment, hurt, and pain
that are almost unbearable, remember that you serve the
One who heals hearts. He knows you best and loves you
most. When the wind is knocked out of you and you feel
as if there is no oxygen left in the room, let God provide
you with the air you need to breathe. Breathe out a prayer
to Him, and breathe in His peace and comfort today.

Lord, be my breath of life, today and always. Amen.

Day 267

LOVE YOUR ENEMIES

*"Love your enemies, do good to them, and lend to
them without expecting to get anything back.
Then your reward will be great."*
LUKE 6:35 NIV

God calls us to a love so brave, so intense that it defies
logic and turns the world on its side. He calls us to
love like He loves. That means we must show patience
where others have been short. We must show kindness
where others have been cruel. We must look for ways
to bless when others have cursed. God promises great
rewards for those who do this. Oh, the rewards may not
be immediate. But when God promises great rewards, we
can know without doubt that any present struggle will
be repaid with goodness and blessing, many times over.

*Dear Father, help me to love those who hate me, bless
those who curse me, and show kindness to those who
have been cruel. Help me to love as You love. Amen.*

Day 268

HIGH EXPECTATIONS

*"They found grace out in the desert.... Israel,
out looking for a place to rest, met God out looking
for them!" GOD told them, "I've never quit loving you
and never will. Expect love, love, and more love!"*
JEREMIAH 31:2–3 MSG

Despite their transgressions, God told the Israelites
He never quit loving them. That is true for you today.
Look beyond any circumstances and you will discover
God looking at you, His eyes filled with love. Scripture
promises an overwhelming, unexpected river of love that
will pour out when we trust the Lord our God. Rest today
in His Word. Expect God's love, love, and more love to
fill that empty place in your life.

*Father, I read these words and choose this
day to believe in Your unfailing love. Amen.*

Day 269

JUNGLE OF LIFE

God's word is alive and working and is sharper than
a double-edged sword. It cuts all the way into us,
where the soul and the spirit are joined, to the
center of our joints and bones. And it judges
the thoughts and feelings in our hearts.

HEBREWS 4:12 NCV

When you take the Bible and live according to God's plans, obeying Him, God's Word cuts like a machete through the entanglements of life. When you choose to use the Sword of Truth, it clears a path and can free you from the weights of the world that try to entrap and ensnare you. No matter what the challenges of life are saying to you today, take His Word and speak His plans into your life. Choose His words of encouragement and peace instead of the negative things life's circumstances are telling you.

God, I want to live in Your truth. I want to believe
what You say about me in the Bible. Help me to
speak Your words today instead of the
problem. Help me believe. Amen.

Day 270

SEASONS OF CHANGE

*The Spirit of God, who raised Jesus from the dead,
lives in you. And just as God raised Christ Jesus
from the dead, he will give life to your mortal
bodies by this same Spirit living within you.*

ROMANS 8:11 NLT

Change can be exciting or fearsome. Changing a habit or moving beyond your comfort zone can leave you feeling out of control. The power of God that formed the world, brought the dry land above the waters of the sea, and raised Jesus from the dead is alive and active today. Imagine what it takes to overcome the natural laws of gravity to put the earth and seas in place. Imagine the power to bring the dead to life again. That same power is available to work out the details of your life.

*Lord, I want to grow and fulfill all You've destined
me to be. Help me to accept change and depend
on Your strength to make the changes
I need in my life today. Amen.*

Day 271

TRIALS

Consider it pure joy, my brothers and sisters, whenever
you face trials of many kinds, because you know that
the testing of your faith produces perseverance.
Let perseverance finish its work so that you may
be mature and complete, not lacking anything.

JAMES 1:2–4 NIV

Things won't be easy and simple until we get to heaven.
So how can we lift our chins and head into tomorrow
without succumbing to discouragement? We remember
God is good. We trust His faithfulness. We ask for His
presence and peace during each moment. We pray for
wisdom and believe the God who holds the universe
in His hands is working every single trial and triumph
together for our good and for His glory.

Lord Jesus, so many troubles are weighing me down.
Help me give You all my burdens and increase
my faith and trust in You. Amen.

Day 272

LOVING SISTERS

*But Ruth replied, "Don't urge me to leave you or
to turn back from you. Where you go I will go,
and where you stay I will stay. Your people
will be my people and your God my God."*

RUTH 1:16 NIV

The story of Ruth and Naomi is inspiring on many levels.
Both women realized their commitment, friendship, and
love for each other surpassed any of their differences.
They were a blessing to each other. Do you have
girlfriends who would do almost anything for you? A
true friendship is a gift from God. Those relationships
provide us with love, companionship, encouragement,
loyalty, honesty, understanding, and more! Lasting
friendships are essential to living a balanced life.

*Father God, thank You for giving us the gift of
friendship. May I be the blessing to my girlfriends
that they are to me. Please help me to always
encourage and love them and be a loving support
for them in both their trials and their happiness.
I praise You for my loving sisters! Amen.*

Day 273

A JOYOUS TREASURE

"The kingdom of heaven is like treasure hidden in a field. When a man found it, he hid it again, and then in his joy went and sold all he had and bought that field."
MATTHEW 13:44 NIV

Have you ever stumbled across a rare treasure—one so priceless you would be willing to trade everything you own to have it? If you've given your heart to Christ, if you've accepted His work on Calvary, then you have already obtained the greatest treasure of all. . .new life in Him. Oh, what immeasurable joy comes from knowing He's placed that treasure in your heart for all eternity!

Father, thank You for the gift of Your Son. Because of Your loving sacrifice, I can forever have joy in my heart. . .knowing I will spend eternity in heaven with You. Amen.

Day 274

O THE DEEP, DEEP LOVE OF JESUS

I pray that out of his glorious riches he may strengthen
you with power through his Spirit in your inner being,
so that Christ may dwell in your hearts through faith.
And I pray that you, being rooted and established in
love, may have power, together with all the Lord's
holy people, to grasp how wide and long and
high and deep is the love of Christ.

EPHESIANS 3:16–18 NIV

What an amazing picture. That He should care for us
in such a way is almost incomprehensible. Despite our
shortcomings, our sin, He loves us. It takes a measure
of faith to believe in His love. When we feel a nagging
thought of unworthiness, of being unlovable, trust in the
Word and sing a new song. For His love is deep and wide.

Lord, thank You for loving me,
even when I'm unlovable. Amen.

Day 275

FOCUS POINT

Therefore. . .stand firm. Let nothing move you.
1 Corinthians 15:58 niv

Some days stress comes at us from all directions. Our emotions are overwhelming. Life makes us dizzy. On days like that, don't worry about getting a lot accomplished—and don't try to make enormous leaps in your spiritual life. Instead, simply stand in one place. Like a ballet dancer who looks at one point to keep her balance while she twirls, fix your eyes on Jesus.

Jesus, when I get caught up in the whirlwind of stress and busyness and my own agenda, I can easily lose my balance. Help me fix my eyes on You. Amen.

Day 276

JOYFUL IN GLORY

Let the saints be joyful in glory:
let them sing aloud upon their beds.
PSALM 149:5 KJV

When do you like to spend time alone with the Lord? In the morning, as the stillness of the day sweeps over you? At night, when you rest your head upon the pillow? Start your conversation with praise. Let your favorite worship song or hymn pour forth! Tell Him how blessed you are to be His child. This private praise time will strengthen you and will fill your heart with joy!

As I enter into this conversation with You,
Father, I praise You. Thank You for being
Lord—and Leader—of my life. Amen.

Day 277

JOY IN THE BATTLE

Then they returned, every man of Judah and
Jerusalem, and Jehoshaphat in the forefront of them,
to go again to Jerusalem with joy; for the LORD
had made them to rejoice over their enemies.

2 CHRONICLES 20:27 KJV

Enemy forces were just around the bend. Jehoshaphat,
king of Judah, called his people together. After much
prayer, he sent the worshippers (the Levites) to the front
lines, singing joyful praises as they went. The battle
was won! When you face your next battle, praise your
way through it! Strength and joy will rise up within you!
Prepare for victory!

No matter what kind of hardship I face, Father God,
I want to praise my way through it and come through
even stronger than I was before. Thank You for helping
me win life's battles, both large and small. Amen.

Day 278

LIKE LITTLE CHILDREN

Some people brought their little children to Jesus so he
could touch them, but his followers told them to stop.
When Jesus saw this, he was upset and said to them,
"Let the little children come to me. Don't stop them,
because the kingdom of God belongs to people
who are like these children. I tell you the truth,
you must accept the kingdom of God as if you
were a little child, or you will never enter it."

MARK 10:13–15 NCV

This passage in Mark tells us that, no matter how old we
are, God wants us to come to Him with the faith of a child.
He wants us to be open and honest about our feelings.
He wants us to trust Him wholeheartedly, just as little
kids do. As adults, we sometimes play games with God.
We tell God what we think He wants to hear, forgetting
He already knows our hearts! God is big enough to handle
your honesty. Tell Him how you really feel.

Father, help me come to You as a little child and be
more open and honest with You in prayer. Amen.

Day 279

WHO EXALTS?

*No one from the east or the west or from the desert
can exalt themselves. It is God who judges:
He brings one down, he exalts another.*

PSALM 75:6-7 NIV

Sometimes we grumble when others are exalted. We feel left out. Why do others prosper when everything around us seems to be falling apart? We can't celebrate their victories. We aren't joyful for them. Shame on us! God chooses whom to exalt. . .and when. We can't pretend to know His thoughts. But we can submit to His will and celebrate with those who are walking through seasons of great favor.

God, it's so hard to be happy for others when I feel like I haven't been blessed in the same way. Please help me to rejoice when others experience Your favor, while I continue to trust that You have a plan for my life—and that Your plan is good! Amen.

Day 280

GRACE IN RETURN

"Then those 'sheep' are going to say, 'Master, what are
you talking about? When did we ever see you hungry
and feed you, thirsty and give you a drink? . . .' Then the
King will say, 'I'm telling the solemn truth: Whenever
you did one of these things to someone overlooked
or ignored, that was me—you did it to me.'"
MATTHEW 25:37–40 MSG

If Christ were sitting on our doorstep, lonely and tired
and hungry, what would we do? We like to think we
would throw the door wide open and welcome Him into
our home. But the truth is we're given the opportunity to
offer our hospitality to Jesus each time we're faced with
a person in need. His grace reaches out to us through
those who feel misunderstood and overlooked, and He
wants us to offer that same grace back in return.

Jesus, open my eyes to the hungry and thirsty
people all around me. Whether their hunger is
spiritual or physical or both—help me to
give them Your grace. Amen.

Day 281

RESCUED!

The LORD wants to show his mercy to you. He wants to rise and comfort you. The LORD is a fair God, and everyone who waits for his help will be happy.

ISAIAH 30:18 NCV

God doesn't want you to feel lonely and unhappy. He waits to bring you close to Him, to comfort you, to forgive you. Wait for Him to rescue you from life's unhappiness. His grace will never let you down. Keep your eyes fixed on Him, and you will find happiness again.

Lord, how I long to receive Your mercy. Draw near to me, rise up and comfort me, and give me happiness in knowing Your help will rescue me. Amen.

Day 282

YOU ARE A WOMAN OF WORTH

A wife of noble character who can find? She is worth far
more than rubies. Her husband has full confidence in
her and lacks nothing of value. She brings him
good, not harm, all the days of her life.
PROVERBS 31:10–12 NIV

Are you the woman of worth that Jesus intends you to be?
We often don't think we are. Between running a household,
rushing to work, taking care of the children, volunteering
for worthwhile activities, and still being a role model for
our families, we think we've failed miserably. Sometimes
we don't fully realize that learning to be a noble woman
of character takes time. Our experiences can be offered
to another generation seeking wisdom from others who
have "been there." You are a woman of worth. God said so!

Father God, thank You for equipping me to be a woman
of noble character. You tell me I am more precious than
jewels, and I claim and believe that wholeheartedly. I
love You, Lord, and I will continue to put You first in my
life. Help me be the woman You intend me to be! Amen.

Day 283

MERCY MULTIPLIED

Mercy unto you, and peace, and love, be multiplied.
JUDE 2 KJV

Have you ever done the math on God's mercy? If so, you've probably figured out it just keeps multiplying itself out, over and over again. We mess up; He extends mercy. We mess up again; He pours out mercy once again. In the same way, peace, love, and joy are multiplied back to us. Praise the Lord! God's mathematics work in our favor.

Father God, I am so thankful Your math works
differently than mine! Amen.

Day 284

PRESSED DOWN, RUNNING OVER

Give, and it shall be given unto you; good measure,
pressed down, and shaken together, and running
over, shall men give into your bosom.

LUKE 6:38 KJV

"Give, and it shall be given unto you." Likely, if you've been walking with the Lord for any length of time, you've heard this dozens of times. Do we give so we can get? No, we give out of a grateful heart, and the Lord—in His generosity—meets our needs. Today, pause and thank Him for the many gifts He has given you. Do you feel the joy running over?

Lord, help me always to give from a grateful heart
and never because I plan to get something in return.
You have given me abundant blessings, Father.
Thank You for always meeting my needs. Amen.

Day 285

ALL OF YOU

*"Love the Lord God with all your passion
and prayer and intelligence and energy."*
MARK 12:30 MSG

God wants all of you. He wants the "spiritual parts," but He also wants your emotions, your physical energy, and your brain's intelligence. Offer them all to God as expressions of your love for Him. Let His grace use every part of you!

*God, I sometimes forget You want all of me. I dedicate
my emotions, my energy, and my intelligence to
You. Enable me to offer these as expressions
of Your love. Amen.*

Day 286

HIS INSTRUMENT

*"The Spirit of the Lord is on me, because he
has anointed me to proclaim good news to the
poor. He has sent me to proclaim freedom
for the prisoners and recovery of sight
for the blind, to set the oppressed free."*

LUKE 4:18 NIV

Just as the Holy Spirit wants you to be free, He also wants
to use you as His instrument to breathe freedom and hope
into the world. Be His instrument today. Tell people the
truly good news that God loves them. Do whatever you
can to spread freedom and vision and hope. Be a vehicle
of the Spirit's grace.

*Lord, I long to be Your instrument. Give me the grace
and wisdom to spread Your message of good news
and freedom to the oppressed. Thank You
for the hope You bring. Amen.*

Day 287

LONGING FOR HOME

*This is what the LORD says: "You will be in Babylon
for seventy years. But then I will come and do
for you all the good things I have promised,
and I will bring you home again."*
JEREMIAH 29:10 NLT

Sometimes in life we go through periods when we feel
out of place, as though we just don't belong. Our hearts
feel restless and lonely. We long to go home, but we
don't know how. God uses those times to teach us special
things we need to know. But He never leaves us in exile.
His grace always brings us home.

*Father, when I am in a season of loneliness and
restlessness, help me trust You to lead me home.
Thank You for Your grace that guides me. Amen.*

Day 288

JOYOUS FREEDOM

Blessed is he whose transgression
is forgiven, whose sin is covered.
PSALM 32:1 KJV

What if you were locked up in a prison cell for years on end? You waited for the day when the jailer would turn that key in the lock—releasing you once and for all. In a sense, experiencing God's forgiveness is like being set free from prison. Can you fathom the joy? Walking into the sunshine for the first time in years? Oh, praise Him for His forgiveness today!

Sweet freedom, Lord. . . It's a beautiful feeling to
have experienced the joy of Your complete and utter
forgiveness. Thank You for setting my spirit free! Amen.

Day 289

ETERNAL JOY!

*And the ransomed of the L*ORD *shall return, and come
to Zion with songs and everlasting joy upon
their heads: they shall obtain joy and gladness,
and sorrow and sighing shall flee away.*
ISAIAH 35:10 KJV

Have you ever pondered eternity? Forever and ever and
ever. . . ? Our finite minds can't grasp the concept, and
yet one thing we understand from scripture—we will
enter eternity in a state of everlasting joy and gladness.
No more tears! No sorrow! An eternal joy fest awaits us!
Now that's something to celebrate!

*When life becomes difficult, help me to keep things
in perspective, Father. The hardships I face in the
day to day are but blips in time compared to
the eternal joy I will experience in heaven.
Thank You for joy that lasts forever. Amen.*

Day 290

FULL!

"I came that they may have and enjoy life,
and have it in abundance [to the full, till it overflows]."
JOHN 10:10 AMP

The life we have in Christ is not restricted or narrow.
Grace doesn't flow to us in a meager trickle; it fills our
life to the fullest. God's grace comes to us each moment,
day after day, year after year, a generous flood that fills
every crack and crevice of our lives—and then overflows.

Jesus, I sometimes long so deeply for heaven
that I forget You have big plans for me on this
earth. Thank You that those plans involve
a rich and abundant life. Amen.

Day 291

HARMONY

The hope of the righteous [those of honorable character and integrity] is joy, but the expectation of the wicked [those who oppose God and ignore His wisdom] comes to nothing.

PROVERBS 10:28 AMP

When we try to live our lives apart from God, we put ourselves in a place where we can no longer see His grace. Joy comes from being in harmony with God.

Father, when I try to live apart from You, gently pull me back into Your arms. Shower me with grace and the joy of living in harmony with You. Amen.

Day 292

WHEN YOU GIVE YOUR LIFE AWAY

Which of you, intending to build a tower,
sitteth not down first, and counteth the cost,
whether he have sufficient to finish it?

LUKE 14:28 KJV

Every person has the same amount of life each day. What matters is how you spend it. It's easy to waste your day doing insignificant things, leaving little time for God. The most important things in life are eternal endeavors. Spending time in prayer to God for others. Giving your life to building a relationship with God by reading His Word and growing in faith. Sharing Christ with others and giving them the opportunity to know Him. These are things that will last. What are you spending your life on? What are you getting out of what you give yourself to each day?

Heavenly Father, my life is full. I ask that You give me wisdom and instruction to give my life to the things that matter most. The time I have is precious and valuable. Help me to invest it wisely in eternal things. Amen.

Day 293

LINKING HEARTS WITH GOD

"You will receive power when the Holy Spirit comes on you; and you will be my witnesses. . .to the ends of the earth."
ACTS 1:8 NIV

God knows our hearts. He knows what we need to make it through a day. So in His kindness He gave us a gift in the form of the Holy Spirit. As a Counselor, a Comforter, and a Friend, the Holy Spirit acts as our inner compass. He upholds us when times are hard and helps us hear God's directions. When the path of obedience grows dark, the Spirit floods it with light. What revelation! He lives within us. Therefore, our prayers are lifted to the Father, to the very throne of God!

Father God, how blessed I am to come into Your presence. Help me, Father, when I am weak. Guide me this day. Amen.

Day 294

THANKFUL, THANKFUL HEART

I will praise you, LORD, with all my heart.
I will tell all the miracles you have done.
PSALM 9:1 NCV

When you choose to approach life from the positive side, you can find thankfulness in most of life's circumstances. It completely changes your outlook, your attitude, and your countenance. When you are tempted to feel sorry for yourself or to blame others or God for difficulties, push PAUSE. Take a moment and rewind your life. Look back and count the blessings God has given you. As you remind yourself of all He has done for you and in you, it will bring change to your attitude and give you hope in the situation you're facing. Count your blessings today.

Lord, I am thankful for my life and all You have done for me. When life happens, help me to respond to it in a healthy, positive way. Remind me to look to You and trust You to carry me through life's challenges. Amen.

Day 295

TRANSFORMED

*And Sarah declared, "God has brought me laughter.
All who hear about this will laugh with me."*
GENESIS 21:6 NLT

The first time we read of Sarah laughing, it was because
she doubted God. She didn't believe that at her age she
would have a baby. But God didn't hold her laughter
against her. Instead, He transformed it. He turned
her laughter of scorn and doubt into the laughter of
fulfillment and grace.

*Father Redeemer, thank You for taking my very worst
moments and transforming them into a story You
can use for Your purpose and Your glory. Amen.*

THE GIFT OF PRAYER

First of all, then, I urge that petitions (specific requests), prayers, intercessions (prayers for others) and thanksgivings be offered on behalf of all people.... This [kind of praying] is good and acceptable and pleasing in the sight of God our Savior.

1 TIMOTHY 2:1, 3 AMP

There is such joy in giving gifts. Seeing the delight on someone's face to receive something unexpected is exciting. Perhaps the absolute greatest gift one person can give to another doesn't come in a box. It can't be wrapped or presented formally; instead, it is the words spoken to God for someone—the gift of prayer. When we pray for others, we ask God to intervene and to make Himself known to them. We can pray for God's plan and purpose in their lives. We can ask God to bless them or protect them. Who would God have you give the gift of prayer to today?

Lord, thank You for bringing people to my heart and mind who need prayer. Help me to pray the things they need from You in their lives. Show me how to give the gift of prayer to those You would have me pray for. Amen.

Day 297

THE RIGHT FOCUS

Turning your ear to wisdom and applying your heart
to understanding—indeed, if you call out for insight
and cry aloud for understanding, and if you look
for it as for silver and search for it as for hidden
treasure, then you will understand the fear of
the LORD and find the knowledge of God.

PROVERBS 2:2–5 NIV

Frustration and stress can keep us from clearly seeing
the things God puts before us. Time spent in prayer
and meditation on God's Word can often wash away
the dirt and grime of the day to day and provide a clear
picture of God's intentions for our lives. Step outside the
pressure and into His presence, and get the right focus
for whatever you're facing today.

Lord, help me avoid distractions
and keep my eyes on You. Amen.

Day 298

HE CARRIES US

In his love and mercy he redeemed them. He lifted
them up and carried them through all the years.
ISAIAH 63:9 NLT

Are you feeling broken today? Depressed? Defeated?
Run to Jesus and not away from Him.

He will carry us—no matter what pain we have to
endure. No matter what happens to us. God sent Jesus to
be our Redeemer. He knew the world would hate, malign,
and kill Jesus. Yet He allowed His very flesh to writhe
in agony on the cross—so we could also become His
sons and daughters. He loves me, and you, that much.

Lord Jesus, thank You for coming to us—for not
abandoning us when we are broken. Thank You for
Your work on the cross, for Your grace, mercy, and love.
Help me to seek You even when I can't feel You, to love
You even when I don't know all the answers. Amen.

Day 299

THE WORD FOR EVERY DAY

As for God, his way is perfect; the word of the Lord is
tried: he is a buckler to all them that trust in him.
2 Samuel 22:31 kjv

God's Word is such an incredible gift, one that goes hand
in hand with prayer. It's amazing, really, that the Creator
of the universe gave us the scriptures as His personal
Word to us. When we're faithful to pick up the Word,
He is faithful to use it to encourage us. Reading and
praying through scripture is one of the keys to finding
and keeping our sanity, peace, and joy.

God, thank You for Your gifts of the holy scriptures and
sweet communion with You through prayer. Amen.

Day 300

STANDING FIRM

I. . .didn't dodge their insults, faced them as they spit in my face. And the Master, God, stays right there and helps me, so I'm not disgraced. Therefore I set my face like flint, confident that I'll never regret this. My champion is right here.
Let's take our stand together!
ISAIAH 50:6–8 MSG

Isaiah reminds us that we are not alone in our battles—even when everyone is against us and we feel outnumbered and outmaneuvered. But remember, your Champion, God, is right there, saying, *"I am not leaving you! We are sticking this out together. You can put your chin up confidently, knowing that I, the Sustainer, am on your side. Let's take our stand together!"*

Lord, boldly stand beside me. May the strength of Your arms gird me as I take a stand for You. Lift my chin today; give me confidence to face opposition, knowing You are right there with me. Amen.

Day 301

STEP BY STEP

*For we walk by faith, not by sight [living our lives
in a manner consistent with our confident
belief in God's promises].*
2 CORINTHIANS 5:7 AMP

The experiences and circumstances of our lives can often
lead us to lose heart. The apostle Paul exhorts us to look
away from this present world and rely on God by faith.
Webster's dictionary defines *faith* as a firm belief and
complete trust. Trusting, even when our faith is small,
is not an easy task. Today, grasp hold of God's Word and
feel His presence. Hold tightly and don't let your steps
falter. He is beside you and will lead you.

*Dear heavenly Father, today I choose to clutch Your
hand and feel Your presence as I trudge the pathways
of my life. I trust You are by my side. Amen.*

Day 302

BIBLICAL ENCOURAGEMENT
FOR YOUR HEART

*Don't be concerned about the outward beauty of fancy
hairstyles, expensive jewelry, or beautiful clothes.
You should clothe yourselves instead with the beauty
that comes from within, the unfading beauty of a gentle
and quiet spirit, which is so precious to God.*

1 PETER 3:3–4 NLT

God is concerned with what is on the inside. He listens
to how you respond to others and watches the facial
expressions you choose to exhibit. He sees your heart.
The Lord desires that you clothe yourself with a gentle
and quiet spirit. He declares this as unfading beauty,
the inner beauty of the heart. Focus on this, and no
one will even notice whether your jewelry shines.
Your face will be radiant with the joy of the Lord, and
your heart will overflow with grace and peace.

*Lord, grant me a quiet and gentle spirit.
I ask this in Jesus' name. Amen.*

Day 303

EVERLASTING LIGHT

*In him was life, and that life was the light of
all mankind. The light shines in the darkness,
and the darkness has not overcome it.*

JOHN 1:4–5 NIV

Focus on the fact that Jesus is the Light of the World
who holds out wonderful hope for us. Set your prayer life
to start with praise and adoration of the King of kings.
Lift your voice in song, or read out loud from the Word.
The Light will eliminate the darkness every time. Keep
your heart and mind set on Him as you walk through the
day. Praise for every little thing; nothing is too small for
God. A grateful heart and constant praise will bring the
Light into your day.

*Dear Lord, how we love You. We trust in You this day to
lead us on the right path lit with Your light. Amen.*

Day 304

ENCOURAGE ONE ANOTHER

*Therefore encourage one another and build each
other up, just as in fact you are doing.*
1 THESSALONIANS 5:11 NIV

Encouragement is more than words. It is also valuing,
being tolerant of, serving, and praying for one another.
It is looking for what is good and strong in a person and
celebrating it. Encouragement means sincerely forgiving
and asking for forgiveness, recognizing someone's
weaknesses and holding out a helping hand, giving
humbly while building someone up, helping others to
hope in the Lord, and praying God will encourage them
in ways you cannot. Whom will you encourage today?
Get in the habit of encouraging others. It will bless them
and you.

*Heavenly Father, open my eyes to those who need
encouragement. Show me how I can help. Amen.*

Day 305

ROPE OF LOVE

*"I led them with cords of human kindness,
with ropes of love. I lifted the yoke from their
neck and bent down and fed them."*

HOSEA 11:4 NCV

God's grace is not a lasso looped around our shoulders,
trapping us and binding us tight. Instead, grace reaches
out to us through the kindness of others. It is a rope of love
that stretches through our lives, leading us to freedom.

*Father, Your Word contains story after story of humans
freed from bondage. I cannot begin to thank You for the
grace that frees me and allows me to thrive. Amen.*

Day 306

FREELY GIVEN

Out of sheer generosity he put us in right standing with himself. A pure gift. He got us out of the mess we're in and restored us to where he always wanted us to be. And he did it by means of Jesus Christ.

ROMANS 3:24 MSG

How kind God has been to us! He brought us close to Himself. He reached down and picked us up out of our messy lives. He healed us so we could be the people we were always meant to be. That is what grace is: a gift we never deserved, freely given out of love.

O kind, gracious, and generous heavenly Father, thank You for the gift of Your Son, for pulling me out of the mess and restoring me to a right relationship with You. Amen.

Day 307

JOYOUS LIGHT

Whom having not seen, ye love; in whom, though now ye
see him not, yet believing, ye rejoice with
joy unspeakable and full of glory.
1 PETER 1:8 KJV

Jesus is the Light of the World. When we accept Him, the light is poured into us. The Holy Spirit comes to reside within, bringing His light. A glorious gift graciously given to us. When we realize the importance of the gift and the blessings that result from a life led by the Father, we can't contain our happiness. The joy and hope that fill our hearts well up. Joy uncontained comes when Jesus becomes our Lord. Through Him, through faith, we have hope for the future. What joy! So let it spill forth in love.

Lord, help me to be a light unto the world,
shining forth Your goodness. Amen.

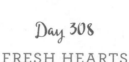

Day 308

FRESH HEARTS

"I will give you a new heart and
put a new spirit within you."
EZEKIEL 36:26 NKJV

Life is full of irritations and hassles. Bills to pay, errands
to run, arguments to settle, and endless responsibilities
all stress our hearts until we feel old and worn. But God
renews us. Day after day, over and over, His grace comes
to us, making our hearts fresh and green and growing.

Lord, when I focus on earthly things, my heart is
small. Expand my heart and give me a heavenly
perspective, knowing You will redeem
and make all things new. Amen.

Day 309

RAISE THE ROOF

*Come, let's shout praises to GOD, raise the roof for
the Rock who saved us! Let's march into his presence
singing praises, lifting the rafters with our hymns!*

PSALM 95:1–2 MSG

Not many had it rougher than King David, who curled
up in caves to hide from his enemies, or Paul in a dark
dungeon cell; yet they still praised God despite the
circumstances. And our God extended His grace to
them as they acclaimed Him in their suffering. The Lord
wants to hear our shouts of joy and see us march into
the courtyard rejoicing. He hears our faltering songs
and turns them into a symphony for His ears. So lift up
your voice and join in the praise to our Creator and Lord.

*Dear heavenly Father, I praise Your holy name.
Bless You, Lord. Thank You for Your grace
and mercy toward me. Amen.*

Day 310

OPEN TO JOY

"The joy of the Lord is your strength."
Nehemiah 8:10 niv

Our God is a God of joy. He is not a God of sighing and gloom. Open yourself to His joy. It is a gift of grace He longs to give you. He knows it will make you strong.

O Lord, Giver of joy and Source of my strength, thank You for these gifts, which are mine in abundance. Help me rely on Your joy and strength. Amen.

Day 311

LOVING SUPPORT

*Let us think of ways to motivate one
another to acts of love and good works.*
HEBREWS 10:24 NLT

Imagine you're sitting in the bleachers watching one of your favorite young people play a sport. You jump up and cheer for him. You make sure he knows you're there, shouting out encouragement. Hearing your voice, he jumps higher, runs faster. That is the sort of excitement and support we need to show others around us. When we do all we can to encourage each other, love and good deeds will burst from us all.

*Lord, help me to be a cheerleader for others.
Help me to see the world through their eyes
and to say and do the things I know would
motivate and encourage them. Amen.*

Day 312

MAGNIFYING LIFE

My soul will make its boast in the Lord; the humble
will hear it and rejoice. O magnify the Lord with
me, and let us exalt His name together!
PSALM 34:2–3 NASB

Mary knew she was the object of God's favor and mercy.
That knowledge produced humility. Try as we might,
we can't produce this humility in ourselves. It is our
natural tendency to be self-promoters...to better our own
reputations. We need the help of the Spirit to remind us
that God has favored each of us with His presence. He
did not have to come to us in Christ, but He did. He has
chosen to set His love on us. His life redeemed ours,
and He sanctifies us. We are recipients of the action of
His grace.

Christ Jesus, help me remember what You have done
for me and desire for others to see and know You. Amen.

Day 313

PRAY ABOUT EVERYTHING

The LORD directs the steps of the godly.
He delights in every detail of their lives.
PSALM 37:23 NLT

The Bible says that the Lord delights in every detail of His children's lives. And no matter how old a believer is, they are and always will be God's child.

Adult prayers don't have to be well ordered and formal. God loves hearing His children's voices, and no detail is too little or dull to pray about. Tell God you hope the coffeehouse will have your favorite pumpkin-spice latte on their menu. Ask Him to give you patience as you wait in line. Thank Him for how wonderful that coffee tastes! Get into the habit of talking with Him all day long, because He loves you and delights in all facets of your life.

Dear God, teach me to pray about everything with
childlike innocence and faith. Amen.

Day 314

EASY AS ABC

*God has done all this, so that we will look for him and
reach out and find him. He isn't far from any of us.*
ACTS 17:27 CEV

God is near. But we must reach out for Him. There's a line
we choose to cross, a specific action we take. We can't ooze
into the kingdom of God; it's an intentional decision. It's
simple, really—as simple as ABC. A is Admitting we're
sinful and in need of a Savior. B is Believing Jesus died
for our sins and rose from the grave. C is Committing
our lives to Him. Life everlasting is then ours.

*God, You are always within reach. For that,
I am so very thankful. I look forward to
eternal life in Your presence. Amen.*

Day 315

TRUST HIM

*"You people who are now crying are blessed,
because you will laugh with joy."*

LUKE 6:21 NCV

God's grace comes to you even in the midst of tears. He
is there with you in your hurt and your sadness. Trust
in Him, knowing sadness does not last forever. One day
you will laugh again.

*Father, even in my darkest days, bestow on me Your
grace. Thank You for the promise that my tears will not
last and that You will replace them with joy. Amen.*

Day 316

HE'S WAITING. . .

"The eyes of the LORD watch over those who do right,
and his ears are open to their prayers."

1 PETER 3:12 NLT

You don't have to try to get God's attention. He is watching you right now. His ear is tuned to your voice. All you need to do is speak, and He will hear you. Receive the gift of grace He gives to you through prayer. Tell God your thoughts, your feelings, your hopes, your joys. He's waiting to listen to you.

Father, what a comfort it is to know You are watching over me and that Your ears are always open to my prayers. Thank You for the gift of Your presence. Amen.

Day 317

WHO HELPS THE HELPER?

The LORD is my strength and my shield; my heart trusted in him, and I am helped: therefore my heart greatly rejoiceth; and with my song will I praise him.
PSALM 28:7 KJV

Helping can be exhausting. The needs of young children, teens, grandchildren, aging parents, our neighbors and fellow church members—the list is never ending—can stretch us until we're ready to snap. And then we find that *we* need help. Who helps the helper? The Lord does. When we are weak, He is strong. When we are vulnerable, He is our shield. When we can no longer trust in our own resources, we can trust in Him. He is always there, ready to help. Rejoice in Him, praise His name, and you will find the strength to go on.

Father, I'm worn out. I can't care for all the people and needs You bring into my life by myself. I need Your strength. Thank You for being my helper and my shield. Amen.

Day 318

NEAR AT HAND

Quiet down before God, be prayerful before him.
PSALM 37:7 MSG

It's not easy to be quiet. Our world is loud, and the noise seeps into our hearts and minds. We feel restless and jumpy, on edge. God seems far away. But God is always near at hand, no matter how we feel. When we quiet our hearts, we will find Him there, patiently waiting, ready to show us His grace.

Lord, when my heart is restless and jumpy, remind me You are near, waiting to comfort me with Your love. Quiet me with Your nearness. Show me Your grace. Amen.

Day 319

IS ANYONE LISTENING?

"And I will ask the Father, and He will give you another
Helper (Comforter, Advocate, Intercessor—Counselor,
Strengthener, Standby), to be with you forever."
JOHN 14:16 AMP

Our heavenly Father wants to hear from us. He cares so
much that He sent the Holy Spirit to be our Counselor,
our Comforter. When we pray—when we tell God our
needs and give Him praise—He listens. Then He directs
the Spirit within us to speak to our hearts and give us
reassurance. Our world is filled with noise and distractions.
Look for a place where you can be undisturbed for a few
minutes. Take a deep breath, lift your prayers, and listen.
God will speak—and your heart will hear.

Dear Lord, I thank You for Your care. Help me
recognize Your voice and listen well. Amen.

Day 320

BEYOND INTELLIGENCE

The fastest runner does not always win the race,
the strongest soldier does not always win the battle,
the wisest does not always have food....
Time and chance happen to everyone.

ECCLESIASTES 9:11 NCV

How smart do you think you are? Do you assume you will be able to think your way through life's problems? Many of us do—but God reminds us some things are beyond the scope of our intelligence. Some days life simply doesn't make sense. But even then, grace is there with us in the chaos. When we can find no rational answers to life's dilemmas, we have no choice but to rely absolutely on God.

God, I am conditioned to rely on strength, speed,
and efficiency. While those things are useful,
I know wisdom is more important. Help me
seek answers directly from You. Amen.

Day 321

ANOTHER MOMENT LONGER

Wait patiently for the LORD. Be brave and courageous.
Yes, wait patiently for the LORD.
PSALM 27:14 NLT

Patience is all about waiting things out. It's about holding on another moment longer. It means enduring hard times. As a younger person, you probably felt you couldn't possibly endure certain things; but the older you get, the more you realize you can. If you just wait long enough, the tide always turns. Hold on. Your life will change. God's grace will rescue you.

Lord, help me wait patiently for You. Help me be brave
and courageous. Remind me the tide always turns
and You will come through for me. Amen.

Day 322

ONE THING IS NEEDED

"Martha, Martha," the Lord answered, "you are worried and upset about many things, but few things are needed—or indeed only one."
LUKE 10:41–42 NIV

We are each given twenty-four hours in a day. Einstein and Edison were given no more than Joseph and Jeremiah of the Old Testament. Since God has blessed each of us with twenty-four hours, let's seek His direction on how to spend this invaluable commodity wisely—giving more to people than things, spending more time on relationships than the rat race. In Luke, our Lord reminded dear, dogged, drained Martha that only one thing is needed—Him.

Father God, oftentimes I get caught up in the minutia of life. The piled laundry can appear more important than the people around me. Help me use my time wisely. Open my eyes to see what is truly important. Amen.

Day 323

NO MORE STING

O death, where is thy sting?
O grave, where is thy victory?
1 CORINTHIANS 15:55 KJV

We have a choice to make. We can either live life in fear or live life by faith. Fear and faith cannot coexist. Jesus Christ has conquered our greatest fear—death. He rose victorious and has given us eternal life through faith. Knowing this truth enables us to face our fears with courage. There is no fear that cannot be conquered by faith. Let's not panic but trust the Lord instead. Let's live by faith and experience the victory that has been given to us through Jesus Christ, our Lord.

Lord, You alone know my fears. Help me trust
You more. May I walk in the victory You
have purchased for me. Amen.

Day 324

THE WHITE KNIGHT

Then I will rejoice in the LORD.
I will be glad because he rescues me.
PSALM 35:9 NLT

We're all waiting for someone to rescue us. We wait and wait and wait. . . . The truth is God doesn't want you to exist in a perpetual state of waiting. Live your life—your whole life—by seeking daily joy in the Savior of your soul, Jesus Christ. And here's the best news of all: He's already done the rescuing by dying on the cross for our sins! He's the *true* white knight who secured your eternity in heaven. Stop waiting; seek His face today!

Jesus, I praise You because You are the Rescuer of my soul. Remind me of this fact when I'm looking for relief in other people and places. You take care of my present and eternal needs, and for that I am grateful. Amen.

Day 325

LOOKING FORWARD

*I focus on this one thing: Forgetting the past
and looking forward to what lies ahead.*
PHILIPPIANS 3:13 NLT

As followers of Christ, we are people who look forward
rather than backward. We have all made mistakes, but
God does not want us to dwell on them, wallowing in
guilt and discouragement. Instead, He calls us to let go
of the past, trusting Him to deal with it. His grace is new
every moment.

*Father, I sometimes ruminate over past mistakes.
Help me not to wallow in the past—instead,
enable me to delight in Your grace,
which is new each moment. Amen.*

Day 326

BRINGING US TO COMPLETION

Being confident of this, that he who began a good
work in you will carry it on to completion
until the day of Christ Jesus.

PHILIPPIANS 1:6 NIV

No matter how many times we fail, no matter how many
times we mess up, we know God hasn't written us off. He's
still working on us. He still loves us. Those of us who
have been adopted into God's family through believing
in His Son, Jesus Christ, can be confident God won't
give up on us. No matter how messed up our lives may
seem, He will continue working in us until His plan is
fulfilled and we stand before Him, perfect and complete.

Dear Father, thank You for not giving up on me.
Help me to cooperate with Your process
of fulfilling Your purpose in me.

Day 327

ACT IN LOVE

Let all that you do be done in love.
1 Corinthians 16:14 nasb

Because love is not merely an emotion, it needs to become real through action. We grow in love as we act in love. Some days the emotion may overwhelm us; other days we may feel nothing at all. But if we express our love while making meals, driving the car, talking to our families, or cleaning the house, God's love will flow through us to the world around us—and we will see His grace at work.

Father, when I feel love, it's easy to show it. But the feelings are not always there. Help me find ways to express Your love obediently through all my actions. Amen.

Day 328

A VERY IMPORTANT PHRASE

And it came to pass...
FOUND MORE THAN 400 TIMES
IN THE KING JAMES BIBLE

There are times in life when we think we can't bear one more day, one more hour, one more minute. But no matter how bad things seem at the time, they are temporary. What's really important is how we handle the opportunities before us today, whether we let our trials defeat us or look for the hand of God in everything. Every day, week, and year are made up of things that "come to pass"—so even if we fail, we needn't be disheartened. Other opportunities—better days—will come. Let's look past those hard things today and glorify the name of the Lord.

Lord Jesus, how awesome it is that You send or allow these little things that will pass. May we recognize Your hand in them today and praise You for them. Amen.

Day 329

SWEET AROMA

The heartfelt counsel of a friend
is as sweet as perfume and incense.
PROVERBS 27:9 NLT

Whether it's over coffee, dessert, or even on the phone, a cherished friend can offer the encouragement and God-directed counsel we all need from time to time. Friendships that have Christ as their center are wonderful relationships blessed by the Father. Through the timely, godly advice these friends offer, God speaks to us, showering us with comfort that is as sweet as perfume and incense. So what are you waiting for? Make a date with a friend and share the sweet aroma of Jesus!

Jesus, Your friendship means the world to me. I value
the close friendships You've blessed me with too!
Thank You for the special women in my life.
Show me every day how to be a blessing to
them, just as they are to me. Amen.

Day 330

NO MATTER WHAT

Be thankful in all circumstances, for this is God's
will for you who belong to Christ Jesus.
1 THESSALONIANS 5:18 NLT

Jesus enables us to be thankful, and He is the cause of our thankfulness. *No matter what happens,* we know Jesus has given up His life to save ours. He has sacrificed Himself on the cross so we may live life to the fullest. And while "to the fullest" means we will experience pain as well as joy, we must *always* be thankful—regardless of our circumstances—for the love we experience in Christ Jesus.

Dear Lord, thank You for Your love. Please let me be
thankful, even in the midst of hardships. You have
blessed me beyond measure. Amen.

Day 331

YOU WILL LIVE

Their past sins will be forgiven, and they will live.
EZEKIEL 33:16 CEV

Do you ever feel doomed? Do you feel as though your mistakes are waiting to fall on your head, like a huge rock that will crush the life out of you? We all have moments like that. But God's grace doesn't let that enormous boulder drop. His forgiveness catches it and rolls it away. You will live after all!

Father, when I am discouraged and beaten down by the past, remind me of Your forgiveness and Your grace. Thank You for Your love that brings me life. Amen.

Day 332

LISTENING CLOSELY

I will listen to what God the LORD says.
PSALM 85:8 NIV

In today's hurried world, with all of the surrounding noise, it's easy to ignore the still, small voice nudging us in the right direction. We fire off requests, expect microwave-instant answers, and get aggravated when nothing happens. Our human nature demands a response. How will we know what to do/think/say if we do not listen? As the worship song "Speak to My Heart" so beautifully puts it, when we are "yielded and still," then He can "speak to my heart."

Listening is a learned art, too often forgotten in the busyness of a day. The alarm clock buzzes; we hit the floor running, toss out a prayer, maybe sing a song of praise, grab our car keys, and are out the door. If only we'd slow down and let the heavenly Father's words sink into our spirits, what a difference we might see in our prayer life. This day, stop. Listen. See what God has in store for you.

Lord, how I want to surrender and seek Thy will.
Please still my spirit and speak to me. Amen.

Day 333

A COMFORTABLE PLACE

*Don't you realize that your body is the temple of the
Holy Spirit, who lives in you and was given to you
by God? You do not belong to yourself.*
1 CORINTHIANS 6:19 NLT

We take the time to make our homes comfortable and beautiful when we know visitors are coming. In the same way, we ought to prepare our hearts for the Holy Spirit, who lives inside of us. We should daily ask God to help us clean up the junk in our hearts. We should take special care to tune up our bodies through exercise, eating healthful foods, and dressing attractively and modestly. Our bodies belong to God. Taking care of ourselves shows others that we honor God enough to respect and use wisely what He has given us.

*Dear Lord, thank You for letting me belong to You.
May my body be a comfortable place for You. Amen.*

Day 334

A CHILD IN NEED

"For all those things My hand has made, and all those things exist," says the LORD. "But on this one will I look: on him who is poor and of a contrite spirit, and who trembles at My word."

ISAIAH 66:2 NKJV

A humble child of God with a need catches His eye. Though He is always watching over all of us, He is drawn to a child who needs Him. We may need forgiveness, wisdom, courage, endurance, patience, health, protection, or even love. God promises to come to our aid when He sees us with a hand up, reaching for His assistance. What needs do you have in your life today? Raise your hand in prayer to God. He'll take care of your needs, and then some—blessing your life in ways you can't even imagine!

Father, thank You for caring about the needs of Your children. Help me remember always to seek You first. Amen.

Day 335

GRACE OF HOSPITALITY

When God's people are in need, be ready to help
them. Always be eager to practice hospitality.
ROMANS 12:13 NLT

God opens Himself to you, offering you everything He has, and He calls you to do the same for others. Just as He made you welcome, make others welcome in your life. Don't reach out to others grudgingly, with a sense of obligation. Instead, be eager for opportunities to practice the grace of hospitality.

Father, although I long to help others in
need, I can sure find a lot of excuses to avoid
practicing hospitality. Please give me an
eagerness to share with others. Amen.

Day 336

A NEW DAY

God, treat us kindly. You're our only hope.
First thing in the morning, be there for us!
When things go bad, help us out!

ISAIAH 33:2 MSG

Every day is a new day, a new beginning, a new chance to enjoy our lives—each day is a new day with God. We can focus on the things that matter most: worshipping Him, listening to Him, and being in His presence. No matter what happened the day before, we have a fresh start to enjoy a deeper relationship with Him: a fresh canvas every twenty-four hours.

Before I get out of bed in the morning, let me say
these words and mean them: "The Lord has
done it this very day; let us rejoice today
and be glad" (Psalm 118:24 NIV).

Day 337

GROWING IN GRACE

This is my prayer for you: that your love will grow
more and more; that you will have knowledge
and understanding with your love.
PHILIPPIANS 1:9 NCV

God wants us to be spiritually mature. He wants us to
love more deeply, and at the same time He wants us to
reach deeper into wisdom and understanding. This is not
something we can accomplish in our own strength with
our own abilities. Only God can help us grow in grace.

God, I long for my love to grow more and more. Fill me
with knowledge and understanding; help me to lean
into Your grace that brings growth. Amen.

Day 338

CHRIST FOLLOWERS

"This is what the Lord All-Powerful says: 'Do what is right and true. Be kind and merciful to each other.'"
ZECHARIAH 7:9 NCV

As Christ's followers, we need to interact with others the way He did when He was on earth. That means we don't lie to each other, and we don't use others. Instead, we practice kindness and mercy. We let God's grace speak through our mouths.

Lord, thank You for the blessing of relationships.
Help me to do what is right and true,
to be kind and merciful to others. Give me Your
grace always. Speak through me. Amen.

Day 339

SLEEP IN PEACE

At day's end I'm ready for sound sleep, for you,
God, have put my life back together.

PSALM 4:8 MSG

At the end of the day, let everything—good and bad together—drop into God's hands. You can sleep in peace, knowing that meanwhile God will continue to work, healing all that is broken in your life. Relax in His grace.

Father, thank You for the gift of rest—a time to put
the busyness aside. When I wake, things make
much more sense. Thank You for putting
my life back together! Amen.

Day 340

UNCHANGED

*Why am I discouraged? Why is my heart
so sad? I will put my hope in God!*
PSALM 42:5 NLT

Thousands of years ago, the psalmist who wrote these
words expressed the same feelings we all have. Some
days we just feel blue. The world looks dark, everything
seems to be going wrong, and our hearts are sad.
Those feelings are part of the human condition. Like
the psalmist, we need to remind ourselves that God
is unchanged by cloudy skies and gloomy hearts. His
grace is always the same, as bright and hopeful as ever.

*Heavenly Father, when I am overcome by sadness,
help me see Your light shimmering just beyond
the clouds. Thank You for Your grace, which is
a bright promise and a great comfort. Amen.*

Day 341

STRONG IN CHRIST

I can do all things through
Christ who strengthens me.
PHILIPPIANS 4:13 NKJV

Left to ourselves, we are weak. We make mistakes. We fall short of our goals. But in Christ we are strong. By His grace we can accomplish anything.

Jesus, I am conditioned to believe that weakness is something to be despised. Help me to see weakness differently—remembering that my weakness is a conduit for Your strength. Amen.

Day 342

TODAY—AND TOMORROW

You are my strong shield, and I trust you completely.
You have helped me, and I will celebrate
and thank you in song.

PSALM 28:7 CEV

God proves Himself to us over and over again. And yet over and over we doubt His power. We need to learn from experience. The God whose strength rescued us yesterday and the day before will certainly rescue us again today. As we celebrate the grace we received yesterday and the day before, we gain confidence and faith for today and tomorrow.

My Father, my Strong Shield, You have proved
Yourself to me over and over again. Remind me
of Your goodness. I praise You and celebrate
Your faithfulness. Amen.

Day 343

OVERFLOWING LOVE

*And may the Lord make your love for one another
and for all people grow and overflow, just as
our love for you overflows.*

1 THESSALONIANS 3:12 NLT

As a very young child, you thought you were the center of the world. As you grew older, you had to go through the painful process of learning that others' feelings were as important as yours. God's grace wants to lift your perspective even higher, though. He wants you to overflow with love for other people.

*Lord, fill my heart with love for others. As I learn to
love You more and receive Your love, may my
love for Your children overflow. Amen.*

Day 344

JOY IN THE MORNING

*All who seek the L*ORD *will praise him.*
Their hearts will rejoice with everlasting joy.
PSALM 22:26 NLT

Every day God provides us with beauty all around to cheer and help us. It may come through the beauty of flowers or the bright blue sky—or maybe the white snow covering the trees of a glorious winter wonderland. It may be through the smile of a child or the grateful face of the one we care for. Each and every day, the Lord has a special gift to remind us of whose we are and to generate the joy we need to succeed.

Lord God, thank You for Your joy; thank You
for providing it every day to sustain me.
I will be joyful in You. Amen.

Day 345

SHARING LIFE

But if we walk in the light, God himself being the light,
we also experience a shared life with one another.
1 JOHN 1:7 MSG

Some of us are extroverts, and some of us are introverts.
But either way God asks us to share our lives in some way
with others. As we walk in His light, He gives us grace to
experience a new kind of life, a life we have in common
with the others who share His kingdom.

Lord Jesus, I recognize You have asked me to share
my life with others. Help me look for opportunities
to make connections as I walk in Your light. Amen.

Day 346

RENEWAL

*"Look, the winter is past,
and the rains are over and gone."*
Song of Solomon 2:11 nlt

Dreary times of cold and rain come to us all. Just as the earth needs those times to renew itself, so do we. As painful as those times are, grace works through them to make us into the people God has called us to be. But once those times are over, there's no need to continue to dwell on them. Go outside and enjoy the sunshine!

Father, it's easy to become discouraged during the long days of winter. But I know times of darkness are necessary to fully appreciate the joy of light. Help me to revel in Your sunlight. Amen.

Day 347

WHAT YOU NEED

Give me neither poverty nor riches!
Give me just enough to satisfy my needs.
PROVERBS 30:8 NLT

God gives us what we need, and He knows exactly what and how much that is. Whatever He has given you financially, He knows that is what you need right now. Trust His grace. He will satisfy your needs.

Father, my Provider, thank You for giving me
exactly what I need. Help me trust You with
Your provision for me and know Your grace
is always enough for me. Amen.

Day 348

WHOLLY AND COMPLETELY

"Forgive others, and you will be forgiven."
LUKE 6:37 NLT

The words *forgive* and *pardon* come from very old words that mean "to give up completely and wholeheartedly." When we forgive others, we totally give up our rights to feel we've been injured or slighted. And in return, God's grace totally fills the gaps left behind when we let go of our own selfishness. As we give ourselves wholeheartedly to others, God gives Himself completely to us.

God, help me forgive others so that nothing hinders me from fully receiving the gift of Your forgiveness. Thank You for Your grace that pours over me. Amen.

Day 349

ALWAYS PRESENT

*LORD, you have been watching. Do not keep
quiet. Lord, do not leave me alone.*
PSALM 35:22 NCV

Have you ever seen a child suddenly look up from playing,
realize she's all alone, and then run to get her mother's
attention? Meanwhile, her mother was watching her all
along. Sometimes solitude is a good thing—and other
times it's just plain lonely. When loneliness turns into
isolation, remember that God's loving eyes are always
on you. He will never leave you all alone, and His grace
is always present.

*Lord, how wonderful to know You are always
with me, watching over me with tender,
loving eyes. Help me listen to Your voice,
remembering I am never alone. Amen.*

Day 350

TO GET THE PRIZE

*Everyone who competes in the
games goes into strict training.*
1 CORINTHIANS 9:25 NIV

We are in the race of life. Time is short, but the days
are long. We have a lot to do, and we never know when
our life will come to an end. All of us are running to the
same finish line. It's important we run our races in a
way that shows we are serious about getting the prize—
eternal life with Christ. We need to show we are running
toward something worth sacrificing for. And we need to
be prepared for whatever falls in our paths—including
other runners.

*Dear God, please help me "run in such a way as
to get the prize" (1 Corinthians 9:24 NIV). Amen.*

Day 351

THRIVE!

*Those who trust in their riches will fall, but the
righteous will thrive like a green leaf.*
PROVERBS 11:28 NIV

Money seems so important in our world. Many things
we want depend on money—that remodeling project
we're hoping to do, the Christmas gifts we want to give,
the vacation we hope to take, and the new car we want to
drive. There's nothing wrong with any of those things,
but our enjoyment of them will always be fleeting. Only
God's daily grace makes us truly grow and thrive.

*Father, remind me that while caring for my family,
making money, and preparing for my future are good
things, they are not my identity. Help me find
my purpose, my worth, in You. Amen.*

Day 352

BACK TO GOD

My dear brothers and sisters, always be willing
to listen and slow to speak. Do not become
angry easily, because anger will not help you
live the right kind of life God wants.

JAMES 1:19–20 NCV

Our feelings are gifts from God, and we should never
be ashamed of them. Instead, we need to offer them all
back to God, both our joys and our frustrations. When
we give God our anger, our irritation, our hurt feelings,
and our frustrations, we make room in our hearts to truly
hear what others are saying.

Father, as uncomfortable as my feelings can be
sometimes, thank You for what they teach me.
Help me trust You with all my feelings so
I can be a good listener. Amen.

Day 353

HEALTHY

"Give us today our daily bread."
MATTHEW 6:11 NIV

We need food each day. Healthy fruits and vegetables, whole grains, lean protein for our bodies—and times of prayer and quiet for our souls. Like a loving mother, God delights in nourishing His children.

Father, You provide everything I need. Help me make wise choices—to fill myself with healthy foods and the nourishment of Your presence. Amen.

Day 354

FAMILY TIES

Jesus, who makes people holy, and those who are made holy are from the same family. So he is not ashamed to call them his brothers and sisters.

HEBREWS 2:11 NCV

You and Jesus are family! Jesus, the One who made you whole and clean in God's sight, is your Brother. Family ties connect you to Him and to all those with whom He is connected. In Christ, we find new connections with each other. By His grace we are now kinfolk.

Jesus, my Brother, how grateful I am to be a part of Your holy family. Thank You for making me whole and clean and for inviting me into Your fold. Amen.

Day 355

ABIDING PEACE

He himself is our peace.
EPHESIANS 2:14 NIV

Regardless of life's circumstances, hope and peace are available if Jesus is there. You do not have to succumb to getting buffeted and beaten by the storms of life. Seek refuge in the center of the storm. Run to the arms of Jesus, the Prince of Peace. Let Him wipe your tears and calm your fears. Like the eye of the hurricane, His presence brings peace and calmness. Move yourself closer. Desire to be in His presence. For He Himself is your peace. As you abide in His presence, peace will envelop you. The raging around you may not subside, but the churning of your heart will. You will find rest for your soul.

Dear Lord, thank You for being our peace in the midst of life's fiercest storms. Amen.

Day 356

MEANT TO MOVE

We are only foreigners living here on earth for a while,
just as our ancestors were. And we will soon be gone,
like a shadow that suddenly disappears.

1 CHRONICLES 29:15 CEV

We are not meant to feel too at home in this world. Maybe
that is why time is designed to keep us from lingering
too long in one place. We are meant to be moving on,
making our way to our forever home in heaven. Grace has
brought us safe thus far—and grace will lead us home.

Father, the old song says, "This world is not my home,
I'm just passing through." How I long for the
treasure of my heavenly home. I cannot
wait to be there with You. Amen.

Day 357

OPEN HOMES

Be quick to give a meal to the hungry,
a bed to the homeless—cheerfully.

1 PETER 4:9 MSG

Because our homes are our private places, the places we retreat to when we're tired to find new strength, it's hard sometimes to open our homes to others. It's bad enough we have to cope with others' needs all day long, we feel, without having to bring them home with us! But God calls us to offer our hospitality, and He will give us the grace to do it joyfully.

God, You have blessed me with a home—a sanctuary.
And I am so grateful for it. Help me share
that blessing joyfully with others. Amen.

Day 358

LIGHT IN THE DARK

The light shines in the darkness,
and the darkness has not overcome it.
JOHN 1:5 NIV

Jesus said in John 12:46 (NIV), "I have come into the world as a light, so that no one who believes in me should stay in darkness." He also promised He is always with us. Because we have Him, we have light. If we fail to perceive it, if we seem to be living in darkness, perhaps we have turned our backs to the light of His countenance. Maybe we are covering our eyes with the cares of this world. Clouds of sin may be darkening our lives, but He has not left us. He promises us that in following Him we will not walk in darkness but have the light of life.

Lord Jesus, show me my blind spots. Where am I
covering my own eyes or walking away from
You? Turn me back to You, the Light of life.

Day 359

STICKING TOGETHER

Families stick together in all kinds of trouble.
PROVERBS 17:17 MSG

Families can drive you crazy. Whether it's the people with whom you share a house or the extended family that gets together at holidays and birthdays, family members can be exasperating, even infuriating. When it comes right down to it, though, your family members are the ones who show you God's grace even when life is hard, the ones who stick by you no matter what (even when they make you crazy!).

Heavenly Father, thank You for my family. Thank You for opportunities to give and receive Your grace. When I am exasperated, remind me of the patience You have with me. Amen.

Day 360

LASTING TREASURE

*"Beware! Guard against every kind of greed.
Life is not measured by how much you own."*
LUKE 12:15 NLT

The Lord never meant for us to be satisfied with temporary treasures. Earthly possessions leave us empty because our hearts are fickle. Once we gain possession of one thing, our hearts yearn for something else. Lasting treasure can only be found in Jesus Christ. He brings contentment so the treasure chests of our souls overflow in abundance. Hope is placed in the Lord rather than our net-worth statement. Joy is received by walking with the Lord, not by chasing some fleeting fancy. Love is showered upon us as we grab hold of real life—life that cannot be bought, but that can only be given through Jesus Christ.

*Dear Lord, may I be content with what You have given
me. May I not wish for more material treasures
but seek eternal wealth from You. Amen.*

Day 361

THE PERFECT REFLECTION

"Give careful thought to your ways."
HAGGAI 1:7 NIV

As we give careful thought to our ways, we should first look back to where we have come from and reflect on God's work in our lives. We are on a journey. Sometimes the road is difficult; sometimes the road is easy. We must consider where we were when God found us and where we are now through His grace. Even more important, we must think about the ways our present actions, habits, and attitude toward God reflect our lives as Christians. Only when we are able honestly to assess our lives in Christ can we call on His name to help perfect our reflection.

Dear Lord, help me look honestly at the ways I live and make changes where necessary. Amen.

Day 362

FOREVER JOY

We don't look at the troubles we can see now....
For the things we see now will soon be gone,
but the things we cannot see will last forever.

2 CORINTHIANS 4:18 NLT

A painter's first brushstrokes look like random blobs—
no discernible shape, substance, or clue as to what the
completed painting will be. But in time, the skilled artist
brings order to perceived chaos. Initial confusion is
forgotten in joyful admiration of the finished masterpiece.
We often can't see past the blobs of trouble on our life
canvases. We must trust that the Artist has a masterpiece
underway. And there will be great joy in its completion.

God, You are the Master Artist. I trust You
to create a masterpiece with my life canvas.

Day 363

AMAZING LOVE

Your unfailing love, O LORD, is as vast as the heavens;
your faithfulness reaches beyond the clouds.
PSALM 36:5 NLT

God loves you. The Creator of the universe cares about you, and His love is unconditional and limitless. You can never make Him tired of you; He will never abandon you. You are utterly and completely loved, no matter what, forever and ever. Isn't that amazing?

O Father, I am so grateful for Your unfailing love,
vast as the heavens, reaching beyond the clouds.
Thank You for never abandoning me and
for Your amazing grace. Amen.

Day 364

EVER WIDER

A longing fulfilled is a tree of life.
PROVERBS 13:12 NIV

Take stock of your life. What were you most hoping to achieve a year ago? (Or five years ago?) How many of those goals have been achieved? Sometimes, once we've reached a goal, we move on too quickly to the next one, never allowing ourselves to find the grace God wants to reveal within that achievement. With each goal reached, His grace spreads out into your life, like a tree whose branches grow ever wider.

God, help me to find the balance between moving forward and looking back. Give me moments to pause and reflect on how far I have come with Your grace. Amen.

Day 365

FINISH LINE

*I have fought the good fight, I have finished
the race, I have kept the faith.*

2 TIMOTHY 4:7 NIV

Paul felt his life was coming to an end. As he wrote to his friend Timothy, he spoke of this. He was not boasting; he was just giving his status report, as it were. Good fight fought? Check. Race finished? Check (well, almost). Faith kept? Check. What does your checklist include? What accomplishments make your list? What goals do you want to be known for achieving? What do you want to do, whom do you want to become, before your race is finished? Write them down today. Put a checkbox by each one. Then go and work out your life, faith, and ministry for all you're worth. Godspeed.

*Dear Lord, bless the work of my hands and feet. Make
me Your servant so that at the end of my life I can look
forward to hearing You say, "Well done." Amen.*

SCRIPTURE INDEX

DAILY INSPIRATION FOR A WOMAN'S SPIRIT!

Read through the Bible in a Year Devotional

This lovely devotional features a simple plan for reading through the Bible in one year with an accompanying devotional thought inspired by that day's Bible reading. Each day's devotion will encourage you to read a passage from the Old Testament, New Testament, and Psalms or Proverbs and provides a relevant spiritual takeaway for practical, everyday living.

Paperback / 978-1-64352-338-5 / $9.99

365 Prayers for a Woman of God

This daily devotional prayer book is a lovely reminder for you to bring any petition before your heavenly Father. And 365 just-right-sized prayers touch on topics that resonate with the hearts of women of all ages and stages. Topics include: Grace, Blessings, Joy, Serving, Contentment, Difficulties, Rest, Surrender, Trust, and more.

Paperback / 978-1-64352-406-1 / $9.99